THE CHRISTIAN MUSICIAN

PIANO · VOCAL · GUITAR

CONTEMPORARY CHRISTIAN HITS

CONTENTS

2	Always Have, Always Will	**Avalon**
11	Between You and Me	**DC Talk**
20	Can't Live a Day	**Avalon**
27	Come Quickly Lord	**Rebecca St. James**
34	Dive	**Steven Curtis Chapman**
42	Don't Look at Me	**Stacie Orrico**
50	Dying to Reach You	**Point of Grace**
58	Fool for You	**Nichole Nordeman**
66	The Glory	**Avalon**
72	God Is God	**Steven Curtis Chapman**
82	Holy	**Nichole Nordeman**
90	I Believe	**ZOEgirl**
106	I Can Only Imagine	**MercyMe**
114	If This World	**Jaci Velasquez**
97	If You Want Me To	**Ginny Owens**
122	Just One	**Phillips, Craig & Dean**
136	A Little More	**Jennifer Knapp**
127	Live Out Loud	**Steven Curtis Chapman**
142	Magnificent Obsession	**Steven Curtis Chapman**
154	Mercy Came Running	**Phillips, Craig & Dean**
160	My Will	**DC Talk**
174	No You	**ZOEgirl**
180	Run to You	**Twila Paris**
188	Song of Love	**Rebecca St. James**
167	Steady On	**Point of Grace**
194	Testify to Love	**Avalon**
203	This Is Your Time	**Michael W. Smith**
210	To Know You	**Nichole Nordeman**
218	Wait for Me	**Rebecca St. James**
226	Wisdom	**Twila Paris**

ISBN 0-634-05451-1

HAL·LEONARD® CORPORATION
7777 W. BLUEMOUND RD. P.O. BOX 13819 MILWAUKEE, WI 53213

For all works contained herein:
Unauthorized copying, arranging, adapting, recording or public performance is an infringement of copyright.
Infringers are liable under the law.

Visit Hal Leonard Online at
www.halleonard.com

ALWAYS HAVE, ALWAYS WILL

Words and Music by GRANT CUNNINGHAM,
TOBY McKEEHAN and NICK GONZALES

Moderately bright

Part of me __ is the pro - di - gal, part of me __ is the oth - er broth - er.
I was born __ with a way - ward heart; still I live __ with the rest - less spir - it.

(Harmony 2nd time only)

© 1999 RIVER OAKS MUSIC CO., ACHTOBER SONGS and VOGON POETRY MUSIC
RIVER OAKS MUSIC CO. and ACHTOBER SONGS Admin. by EMI CHRISTIAN MUSIC PUBLISHING
All Rights Reserved Used by Permission

(Harmony 2nd time only)
But I ___ think the heart of me is real-ly some-where be-tween __ them.
My soul __ is so well worn you'd think I'd have ____ ar-rived by now.

(Harmony both times)
Some days __ I'm run-ning wild, some days __ we're re-con-ciled.
I'm caught in the trap-pings of my search for a last-ing love.

(Harmony 2nd time only)
But I won-der all __ the while __ why you put __ up with me, ___ when
I've made mis-takes __ e-nough to last me __ a life-time.

I wres-tle most __ days __ to find __ ways __ to
Still slip, __ I still __ fall. __ But I'll ___ al-ways

do as I please. / run back to you. I always have. I always will. You saved me once. You save me still. A longing heart Your love alone can fill. You always have, always will.

(Spoken:) You always have.

You always will. will.

I'm gon-na keep trust-ing You.

I'm gon-na keep trust-ing You.

I see what You've seen me through.

I see what You've seen me through.

I'm go - in' where You have gone.

I'm go - in' where You have gone, _____ yeah. _____

I'm let - ting You lead me, I'm let - ting You lead me home. _____

I'm let - ting You lead me home. _____

All my _____ days, _____ Al - ways _____ and _____ for - ev - er. _____

Never leave me, never, never far, ever love me, ever, here I'll stay. Here's my heart. I'll always love you.

Am7
C
G
Am
Love you yeah yeah. I
C
G
Am
always have. I always will. You saved
F
C
F
G
me once. You save me still. My long-
Am7
F
C
ing heart your love alone can fill.

F C G
You always have
Oh.
I
C G Am
always have. I always will. You saved
F C F G
me once. I know you'll save me still. My long-
Oh.
Am7 F C
-ing heart your love alone can fill.

| F | C | G |

You al - ways have, ____ al - ways

| C | Am |

will. _____ Oh, _____ you al -

| C | Am |

-ways will. ___ You al - ways ___ will. ___

Csus2

BETWEEN YOU AND ME

Words and Music by TOBY McKEEHAN
and MARK HEIMERMANN

Medium Pop Rock

Sor-row is a lone-ly feel-ing,
Con-fes-sion is the road to heal-ing,
un-set-tled is a pain-ful place.
for-give-ness is the prom-ised land.

© 1995 UP IN THE MIX MUSIC, ACHTOBER SONGS and FUN ATTIC MUSIC
UP IN THE MIX MUSIC and ACHTOBER SONGS Admin. by EMI CHRISTIAN MUSIC PUBLISHING
All Rights Reserved   Used by Permission

| E(add2) | Bm7 | A(add2) |

I've lived with both for far too long now since we've part-ed ways.
I'm reach-ing out in my con - vic - tion, I'm long-ing to make a - mends.

| Am7 | E(add2) | Bm7 |

I've been wres-tl-ing with my con - science and I
So I'm sor-ry for the words I've spo - ken, for

| A(add2) | Am | C |

found my-self to blame. If there's to be an-y res-
I've be-trayed a friend. We've got a love that's worth

Cm7
3 fr
C
- o - lu - tion, I've got to peel my pride
pre - serv - ing and a bond I will
Cm7
3 fr
Dm11
5 fr
G(add2)
a - way.
de - fend.
Just be - tween you and me
Em9
E♭maj7
3 fr
F(add2)
I've got some-thing to say, wan - na get it straight be - fore the sun goes down.

| G(add2) | Em9 | E♭maj7 |

Just be-tween you and me con-fes-sion needs to be made, ___ rec-om-pense is my way ___

| Dm11 | C(add2) | G(add2) | Csus2 | C(add2) |

___ to free-dom now. Just be-tween you and me I've got some-thing to say. ___

1.
F6/9

If con-

2.
F6/9

15

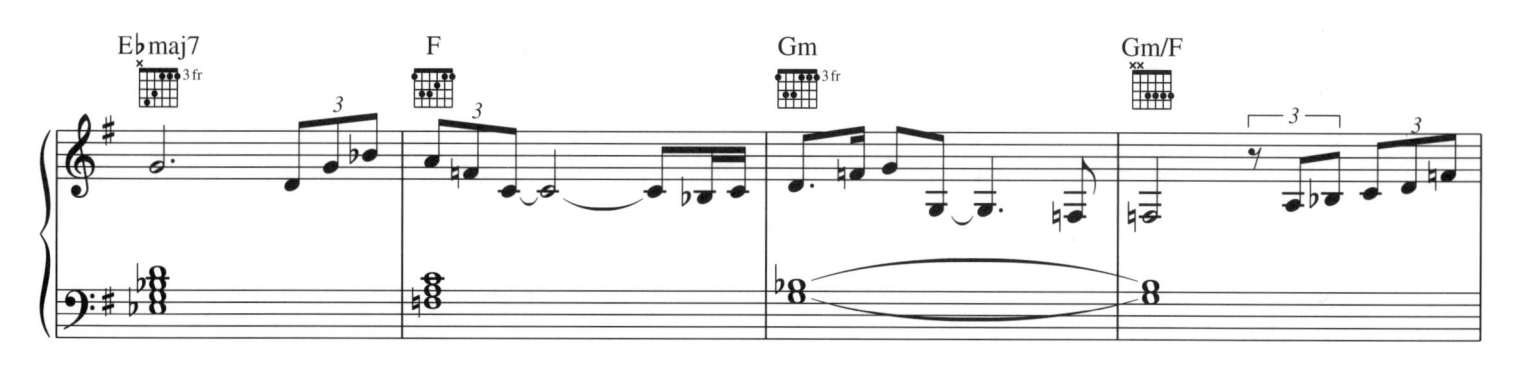

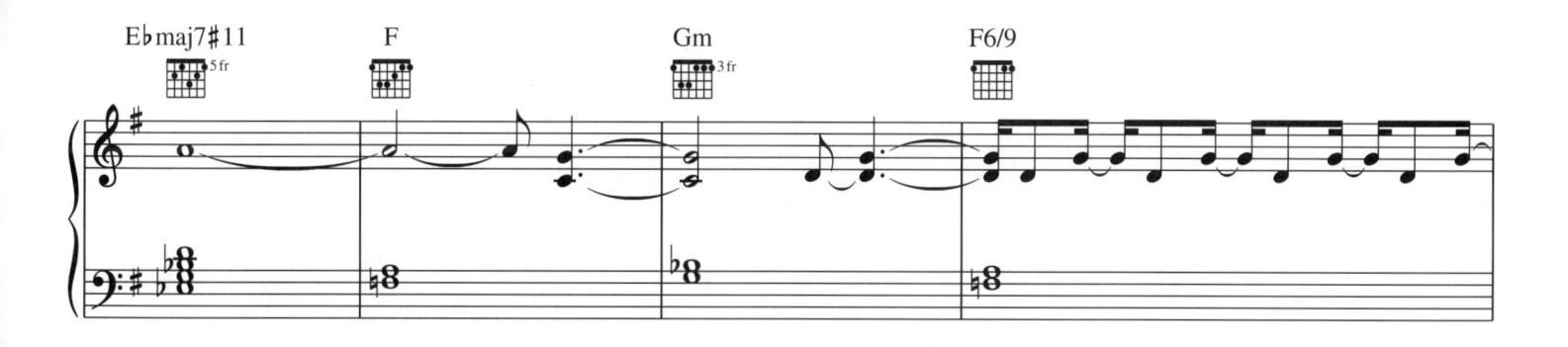

In my pur-suit of God, I thirst for ho-li-ness, as I ap-proach the Son, I must con-sid-er this. Of-fens-es un-re-solved, they'll keep me from the throne.

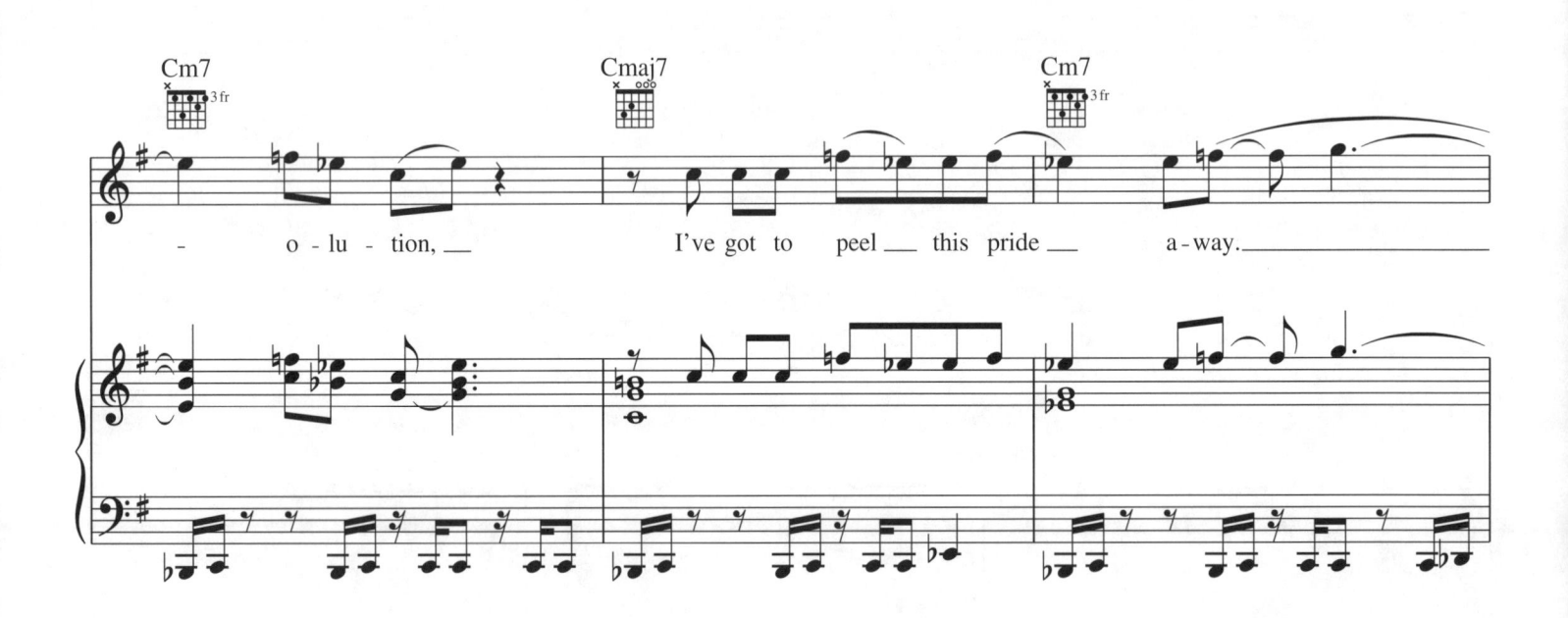

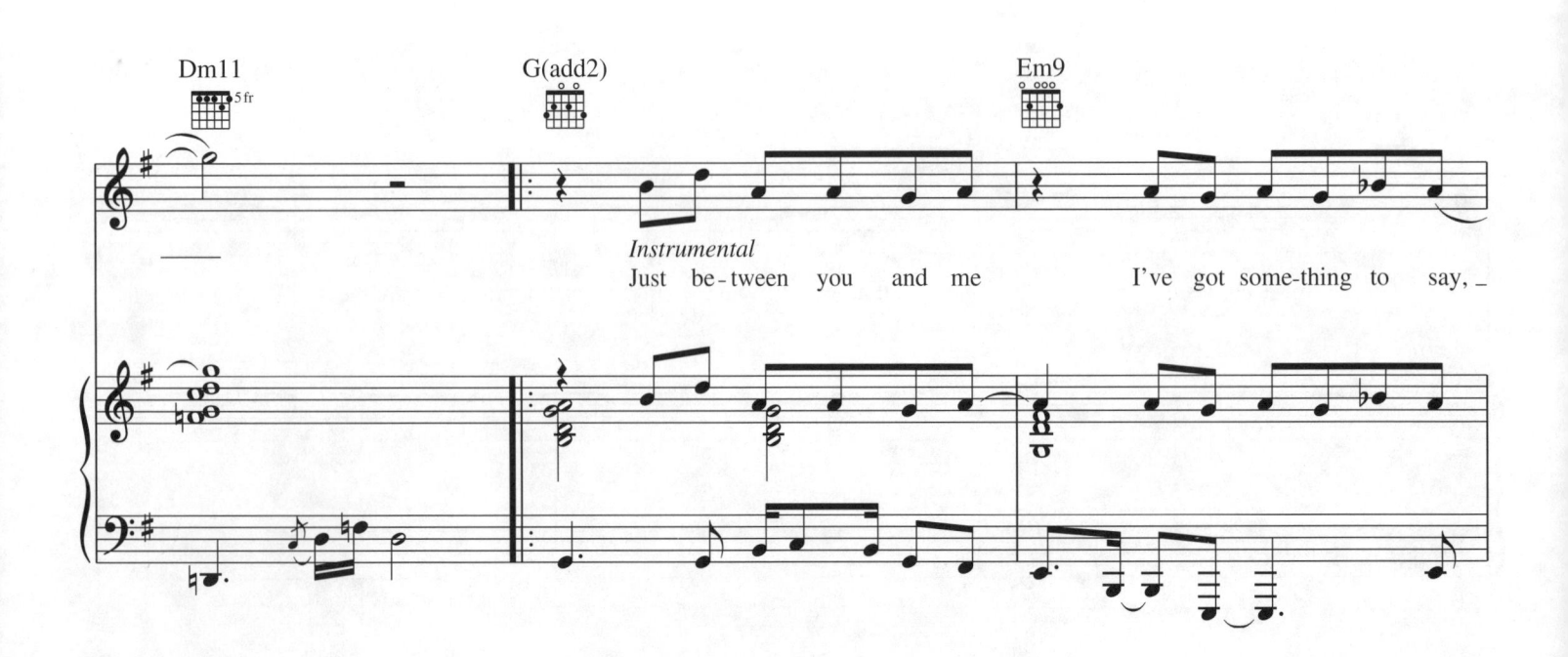

Be-fore I go to Him my wrong must be a - toned. If there's to be an-y res- o-lu-tion, I've got to peel this pride a-way.

Instrumental
Just be-tween you and me I've got some-thing to say,

wan-na get it straight before the sun goes down. Just be-tween you and me

con-fes-sion needs to be made, rec-om-pense is my way to free - dom.

End instrumental

It's my way to free - dom.

F6/9
G
Em7
(It's my way to free - dom, it's my way to free - dom.)
Ebmaj7
Dm11
C(add2)
G
I've got some-thing to say, so let me say it to - day.
(It's my way to free - dom, it's my
Em7
Ebmaj7
Fsus2
I've got some-thing to say, con - fes - sion needs to be made.
way to free - dom.)
(It's my

way to free - dom, it's my way to free - dom.) _____ I've got some-thing to say,

con - fes - sion needs to be made. _____
(It's my way to free - dom, it's my way to free - dom.) _____ I've got

some-thing to say, a - ha, a - ha.

Can't Live A Day

Words and Music be CONNIE HARRINGTON,
JOE BECK and TY LACY

Slowly

I could live life alone and never fill the longings of my heart, the healing warmth of someone's arms. And I
could travel the world, see all the wonders beautiful and new. They'd only make me think of You. And I

(Harmony 2nd time only)

could live without dreams, and never know the thrill
could have all life offered, riches that were far

Copyright © 1999 by BMG Songs, Inc., Ariose Music and Bridge Building Music (a div. of Brentwood-Benson Music Publishing, Inc.)
All Rights for Ariose Music Administered by EMI Christian Music Publishing
International Copyright Secured   All Rights Reserved

of what could be with ev-'ry star so far and out of reach.
be-yond com-pare, to grant my ev-'ry wish with-out a care.

I could live with-out man-y things and I
Oh, I could do an-y-thing. Oh, yes. But if

could car-ry on. But I
You weren't in it all, I } could-n't face my life to-mor-row with-out Your hope

(Harmony 2nd time only)
in my heart. I know I can't live a day with-out You.

22

Lord, there's no night and there's no morning without Your loving arms to hold me. You're the heartbeat of all I do. I can't live a day without You. No no. And oh, I Oh, Je-

-sus, I live because You live. You're like the air I breathe. Oh, Je-sus, Oh, I have because You gave. You're ev-er-y-thing to me. Oh, I could-n't face

...my life tomorrow without Your hope in my heart. I know I can't live a day without You. Oh Lord, there's no night and there's no morning without Your loving arms to hold me. You're the...

I can't live a day without You. heartbeat of all I do. I couldn't face my life tomorrow without Your hope in my heart. I know, I know. Hey hey. Lord, there's no night can't live a day without You. There's no night and there's no morn-ing. and there's no morn-ing with-out Your lov-ing arms to hold me. You're the heart-beat of all I do. I can't live a day with-out You. No. Oh. Oh.

COME QUICKLY LORD

Words and Music by REBECCA ST. JAMES
and DAVID SMALLBONE

*Vocal line written one octave higher than sung

© 1998 UP IN THE MIX MUSIC, BIBBITSONG MUSIC (BMI) and SAY IT LOUD MUSIC (ASCAP)
UP IN THE MIX MUSIC Admin. by EMI CHRISTIAN MUSIC PUBLISHING
BIBBITSONG MUSIC and SAY IT LOUD MUSIC Admin. by ICG
All Rights Reserved   Used by Permission

B
Amaj7
B6
soon. And I long so much to see You that I
sleep-ing. And I long so much to see You that I
C♯m11
Emaj7/G♯
Amaj9
B
cry. Ev - 'ry - where are the signs
reach for the skies. And I lift up my hands
F♯sus2
G♯7
that the end is near. I say come quick -
and I hold them high, high. Come quick -
E
Bsus
C♯m7
- ly, Lord,
- ly, Lord,
when the sun grows dark and the moon

will shine no more. Quick-ly, Lord, when the stars fall out of the sky a-bove. Won't You come, dear Lord? Be

30

G♯m7(add4)/B♯
2 fr
Amaj7
B6
(Come take us a - way
for me. Come quick - ly,
Cdim7
C♯m
4 fr
Amaj7
to be with You. Come
quick - ly.
B6
F♯m
G♯sus
take us a - way.)
E
B(add4)
C♯m
4 fr

E5/D
E/A
E
2 fr
Bsus
Cdim7
E
Come quick - ly, Lord,
Bsus
C♯m7
E/D
4 fr
when the sun grows dark and the moon will shine no more. Quick -
E/A
E
Bsus
- ly, Lord, when the stars fall out of the sky

1
Cdim7
2
Cdim7
E
a - bove. Quick- a - bove. Come,
B5
C♯m
4 fr
D(add2)
take us a - way to be with You. Come
E/A
E
Bsus
2 fr
take us a - way.
Repeat and Fade
Cdim7
Optional Ending
Cdim7
Bsus
2 fr
E

DIVE

Words and Music by
STEVEN CURTIS CHAPMAN

Moderately fast

The long a-wait-ed rains have fall-en hard up-on the thirst-y ground;
There is a su-per-nat-ral pow-er in this might-y riv-er's flow.

© 1999 SPARROW SONG and PEACH HILL SONGS
Admin. by EMI CHRISTIAN MUSIC PUBLISHING
All Rights Reserved   Used by Permission

C♭maj7
D♭
they've carved their way to where the wild and rush - ing riv - er can be found.
It can bring the dead to life and it can fill an emp - ty soul
C♭maj7
D♭
And like the rain I have been car - ried here to where the riv - er flows,
and give our heart the on - ly thing worth liv - ing and worth dy -
E♭
A♭sus2
G♭
C♭maj7
yeah.
- ing for, yeah.
D♭
My heart is rac - ing and my knees are weak as I walk to the edge.
But we will nev - er know the awe - some pow - er of the grace of God

I know there is no turn-ing back a-once my feet have left the ledge.
un-til we let our-selves get swept a-way in-to this ho-ly flood.

And in the rush, I hear a voice that's tell-ing me it's time to take
So if you take my hand, we'll close our eyes and count to three and take

the leap of faith, so here I go. *I'm div-ing in; I'm go-ing deep,*
the leap of faith. Come on, let's go.

in o-ver my head. I wan-na be caught in the rush, lost in the flow.

In o-ver my head I wan-na go. The riv-er's deep; the riv-er's wide;

the riv-er's wa-ter is a-live, so sink or swim, I'm div-ing in.

2
Eb
3fr
Bb
Ab
4fr
I'm_ div - ing in._
Eb
3fr
Bb
Ab
4fr
Oh,
I'm div - ing in,_
Eb
3fr
Bb
Ab
4fr
yeah, hah.
I'm div - ing in,_
Eb
3fr
Bb
Ab
4fr
yeah,
here I
go.

Come on, __ let's go. __ I'm div - ing in; I'm go - ing deep, in o-ver my head. I wan-na be caught in the rush, lost in the flow

in o-ver my head I wan-na go. The riv-er's deep, the riv-er's wide,

the riv-er's wa-ter is a-live. So sink or swim, I'm div-ing in.

So sink or swim, I'm div-ing in. So sink or swim,

41

DON'T LOOK AT ME

Words and Music by STACIE ORRICO
and MARK HEIMERMANN

Moderate 16th-note Shuffle

Don't look at me if you're lookin' for per- fec- tion. Don't look at me; I will on- ly let you down. I'll do my best to point you in the right dir- ec- tion, but don't look at me, no, no, no,

© 2000 STARSTRUCK MUSIC and FUN ATTIC MUSIC
STARSTRUCK MUSIC Admin. by EMI CHRISTIAN MUSIC PUBLISHING
All Rights Reserved   Used by Permission

don't look at me; look at Him. Some-times I have a fear that you will see a mirror and get the thought that it's the main at-trac-tion. But all that you de-tect is just what I re-flect of the ob-ject of my own af-fec-tion. I'll lead you to the One I found;

He'll give you ev-'ry-thing you need. Don't look at me if you're lookin' for per-fec-tion. Don't look at me; I will only let you down. I'll do my best to point you in the right di-rec-tion, but don't look at me, no, no, no, don't look at me; look at Him.

It's un-der-stand-a-ble to want a he-ro, but peo-ple can't meet all your ex-pec-ta-tions. Still, some can teach you things a-bout the love He brings; just know, the source if life is in the Sav-ior. I'll lead you to the one I found; He'll give you ev-'ry-thing you need._____ Don't look at me if you're lookin' for perfection. Don't look at me; I will only let you down. I'll do my best to point you in the right direction, but don't look at me, no,___ no, no,___ don't look at me.

He's the one who lived a perfect life; He's the one who always gets it right.___

[C#m] He's the one and only guiding light; **[D#dim]** **[E6]** oh, **[F#7]** yeah.

[C#m] He is ev-'ry-thing you want to be; **[Cdim]** **[C#m/B]** He's the answer to your ev-'ry **[Bbm7b5]** need.

[A] If you follow Him, then you will see **[G#7]** He's like no other, _____

_____ yeah. _____ **[A]** **[Cdim]** **[C#m]** Ooh, _____ **[E6]** ooh, _____

47

48

Lyrics:
ooh. Yeah. I'll do my best to point you in the right di- rec-tion; but don't look at me, no, no, no. Don't look at me. Don't look at me. (I'll only let you go.) I'll do my

best to point you in the right di - rec - tion; but don't look at me, no, ____ no, no, don't look at me, look at Him.

DYING TO REACH YOU

Words and Music by MICHAEL PURYEAR
and GEOFFREY THURMAN

Moderately

He looked through tem-ples of time to see you right where you stand.
He's stand-ing there at the door; you can hear Him call you by name.

He emp-tied all of Him-self
He sim-ply waits to for-give

Copyright © 1994 by Careers-BMG Music Publishing, Inc., Final Four Music, P.E. Velvet Music (a div. of Harding Music Group) and Seventh Son Music, Inc. (a div. of Glen Campbell Music)
All Rights for Final Four Music Administered by Careers-BMG Music Publishing, Inc.
International Copyright Secured   All Rights Reserved

so He could reach out His hand
all of the guilt and the shame.

to give hope and meaning
He gave up His own life,

to the wasted away.
and He still bears the scars.

And you are one of the ones
He only wants to receive

that He was dy-ing to save. Oh,
you, so come as you are.

yeah. He was dy-ing to reach you,

try-ing to meet you where you need Him most. You've been

liv-ing in search of the

whole truth and real love your whole life through. You can o-pen your heart, 'cause He's dy-ing to reach you.

dy-ing to reach you.

Oh, He has waited time and time before. You must be still and know that He is Lord. He was dying to reach you, trying to meet you where you need Him the most. Tell me, what are you look-ing for? Won't you o-pen your heart? He's dy-ing to reach you, dy-ing to reach you, try-ing to meet you where you

need Him most. You've been living in search of the whole truth and real love your whole life through. You can open your heart 'cause He's dying to reach you. (Dying to reach you.)

Dy - ing to reach you,

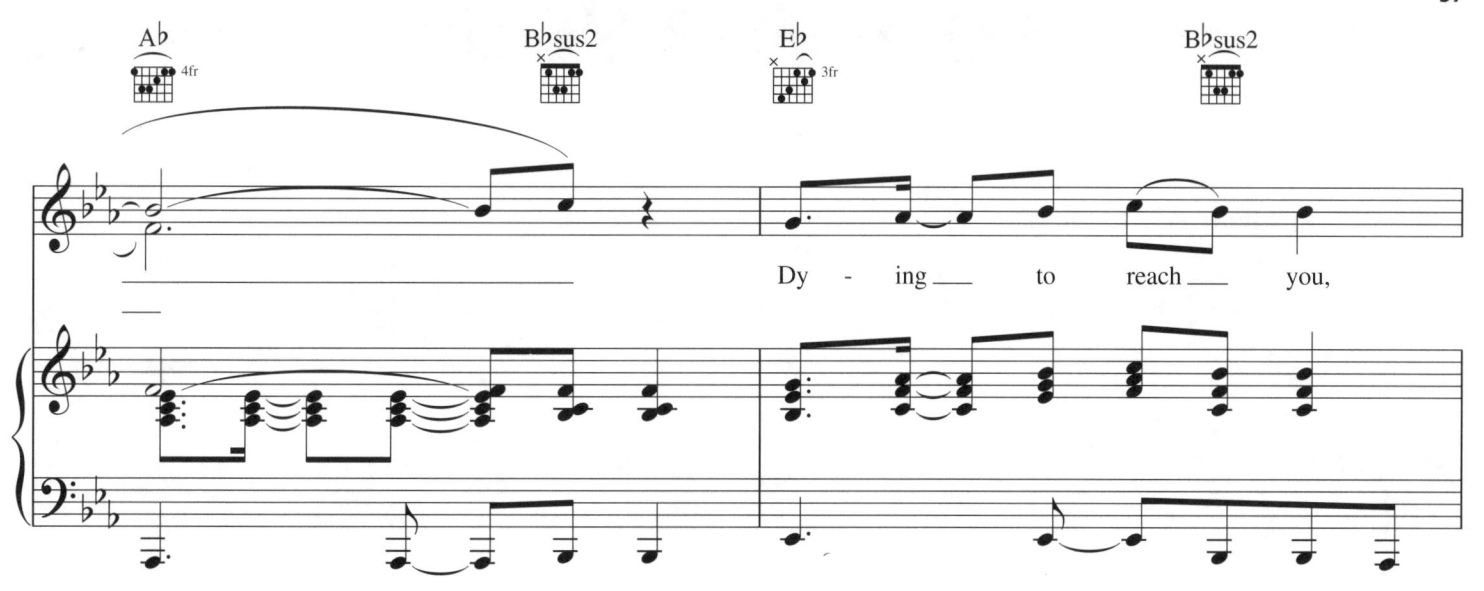

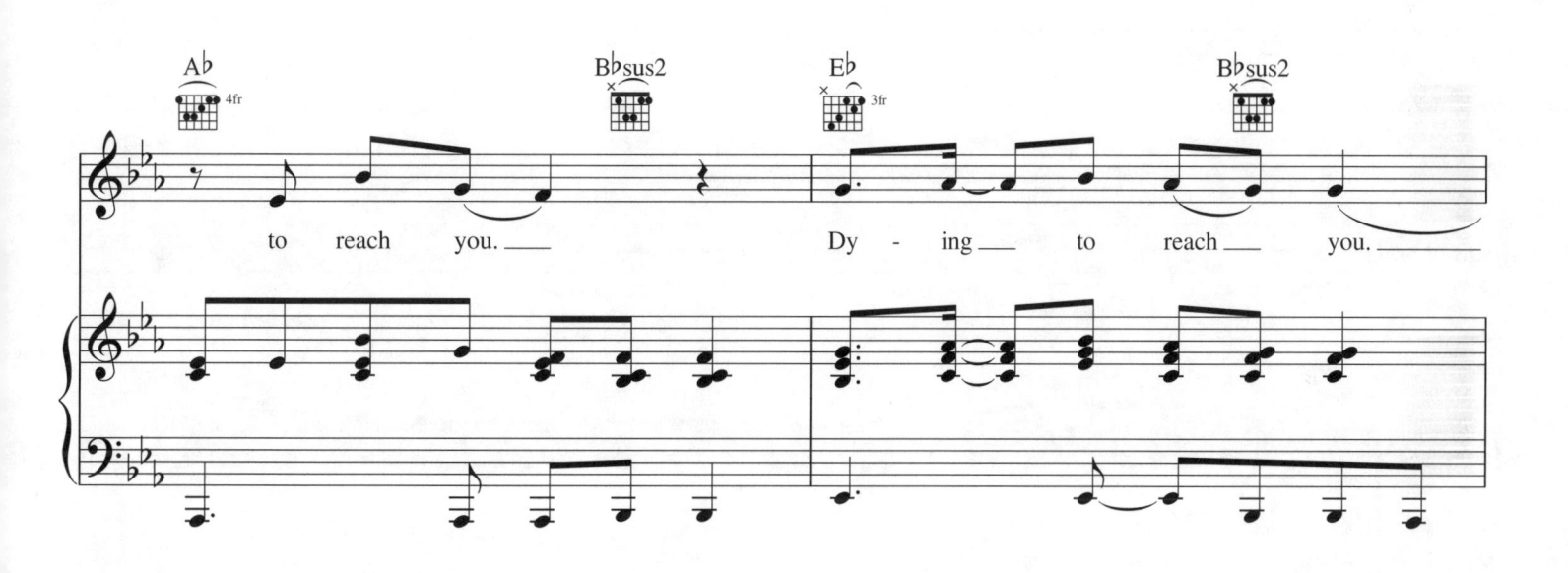

to reach you. Dy - ing to reach you.

FOOL FOR YOU

Words and Music by
NICHOLE NORDEMAN

Moderately bright

There are times when faith and com-mon sense do not a-lign,
I ad-mit that in my dark-est hours I've asked, "What if?"

when hard-core ev-i-dence of You is hard to find.
What if we cre-a-ted some kind of man-made faith like this?

© 2000 ARIOSE MUSIC
Admin. by EMI CHRISTIAN MUSIC PUBLISHING
All Rights Reserved Used by Permission

And I __ am si - lenced in __ the face __ of ar - gu - men - ta - tive __ de - bate __ and
Out __ of good __ in - ten - tion or e - mo - tion - al __ in - ven - tion

it's a long __ hill, __ it's a lone - ly climb. __ 'Cause they __ want proof. __
and af - ter life is through there __ will be __ no You. __

They want proof __ of all __ these mys - ter - ies __ I claim, __
'Cause they want proof __ of all __ these mir - a - cles __ I claim, __

'cause on - ly fools __ would want __ to chant __ a dead __ man's
'cause on - ly fools __ be - lieve _ that men __ can walk __ on

A♭sus2
B♭7sus
name.
waves.
May - be it's true, yeah.
E♭
B♭
Cm
A♭
I would be a fool for You.
E♭
B♭
Cm
A♭sus2
All be - cause You asked me to. A
A♭m6/C♭
A♭m6
B♭7sus
sim - ple - ton who's seem - ing - ly na - ive. I do be -

lieve You came and made Yourself a fool for me.

Unaware of popularity,

un - con - cerned with dig - ni - ty, You made _____ me _____ free. _____ That's proof e - nough for me. _____

Ah. _____

Eb
Bb
Cm7
Absus2
I would be a fool for You.
Eb
Bb
Cm
Ab
On - ly if You asked me to. A
Abm/Cb
Abm6
Bb7sus
sim - ple - ton who's on - ly think - ing of the cause of
Eb
Bb
Cm
Absus2
love. I will speak Je - sus' name.

| Eb | Bb | Cm | Absus2 |

If that makes me cra-zy, they can call me crazed. I'm

| Abm6/Cb | | Abm6 | Bb7sus |

hap-py to be seem-ing-ly na-ive. I do be-

| Abm6/Cb | Dbsus2 | Eb/Ab | Eb/G |

lieve You came and made Your-self a fool for me.

| Fm11 | Eb | Eb/Ab | Eb/G |

Ah.

Fm11
E♭
E♭(add4)
E♭
3 fr
9 fr
Fm11/E♭
E♭
E♭(add4)
E♭
A fool for You.
Ah.
Fm11/E♭
E♭
E♭(add4)
E♭
Fm11/E♭
E♭
E♭/A♭
E♭/G
Fm11
Do do do do do do.

THE GLORY

Words and Music by REGIE HAMM
and JIM COOPER

Moderately slow

Female: In the sol-i-tar-y mo-ment of His birth on this bar-ren dust-y land, all of heav-en kissed the face of the earth. With a mir-a-cle of Love,

Copyright © 1999 Designer Music Group, Inc. (SESAC), Minnie Partners Music (SESAC)
(both admin. by Brentwood-Benson Music Publishing, Inc.), Boisseau Music Publishing (BMI),
Jimmy Vision Music (BMI) (both admin. by ICG) and Songs of Lehsem (SESAC)
Songs of Lehsem Administered by Music & Media International, Inc.
International Copyright Secured   All Rights Reserved

B
C♯m
G♯m/B
4 fr
God be - came a man, but He was sent a - way to
tried to find sal -
F♯sus
F♯
draw His fi - nal breath when He was on - ly thir - ty - three.
va - tion on my own in a search for some - thing real.
And in the shame of dy - ing a
There's a guil - ty heart in -
A
crim - i - nal's death He cleansed an an - gry world and in His
side this flesh and bone. I fall up - on His grace and

B E A
suf - fer - ing I see
I be - gin to feel
the glo - ry of the blood,
cresc.
f
B A G# C#m C#m/B
the beau - ty of the Bod - y that was bro -
4 fr
A E/B B E A/C#
- ken for our for - give - ness. The glo - ry of His per -
E/B A C#m B
- fect Love is the heart of the sto - ry, the glo -

A
B
C♯m
4 fr
F♯sus
F♯
- ry of the Blood.
Male: I have
mp
E
C
D/C
Male: And when I close my eyes I can
C
D/C
Em
D/E
see Him hang - ing there.
Female: Oh, the pre - cious wound - ed Lamb
Em
D/E
C
D/C
of God!
Both: And all the maj - es - ty in this

world can not __ com - pare __ to the glo - ry. _____

Male: The beau - ty of ____ the bod - y that was

Both: bro - ken for our for-give - ness. The glo - ry of ___ the Blood, __

_____ the beau - ty of ____ the Bod - y that was

broken for our for-give-ness. The glo-ry of__ His per - fect love__ is the

heart of the sto - ry, the glo - ry__ of_____ the blood._____

Male: He was sent a - way_____ to

draw His fi - nal breath.__ *Both:* when He was on - ly thir - ty - three.__

GOD IS GOD

Words and Music by
STEVEN CURTIS CHAPMAN

Moderately

And the pain falls like a cur- tain on the things I once called certain, and I have to say the words

-der, and I'm filled with awe and wonder, 'til the only burning

Original key: D♭ major. This edition has been transposed up one half-step to be more playable.

© 2001 SPARROW SONG and PEACH HILL SONGS
Admin. by EMI CHRISTIAN MUSIC PUBLISHING
All Rights Reserved   Used by Permission

Bm(add2) ... I fear the most: "I just don't know."
ques - tion that re - mains is, "Who am I?"

Asus2

Gsus2
And the ques - tions with - out an -
Can I form a sin - gle moun -

Bm(add2)
- swers come and par - a - lyze
- tain? Take the stars in hand

Gsus2
the danc - ers, so I stand here on the
and count them? Can I e - ven take a breath

74

| Bm(add2) | Asus2 |

stage a-fraid to move, a-fraid to fall,
with-out God giv-ing it to me?

| Gsus2 | D/F# |

oh, but fall I must on this
He is first and last be-fore

| F6/9 | B♭maj9 |

truth that my life has been formed from the dust.
all that has been, be-yond all that will pass.

| Dsus2 | Dmaj9 |

God is God and I am not.

75

it all, for on-ly God is God.

1. And the sky be-gins to thun-

2. (Great is the Lord, ho-ly, ho-ly, great is the Lord, oh.

Great is the Lord, ho-ly, ho-ly,

great is ____ the Lord.)

Oh, ___ how

great are the rich-es of His wis-dom and know-ledge, how un-search - a - ble, for to Him and through Him and from Him are all things. So let us wor-ship be-

fore the throne of the One who is worthy of worship a - lone. Oh, God, God is God and I am not. I can on - ly see a part of the pic - ture __ He's paint - ing. __

God, __ God is God and I am __ man, __ so I'll nev - er un - der - stand __ it all, __ for on - ly God __ is God. __

On - ly God is __ God. __

(Great is __ the Lord.   Great is __ the Lord.

Ho - ly, ho - ly, great is __ the Lord.)

Repeat and Fade

Optional Ending

HOLY

Words and Music by NICHOLE NORDEMAN
and MARK HAMMOND

E♭5
A♭sus2
- el before I walked down one that led me
D♭6/9
D♭maj9
D♭sus2
to You? And how man - y dreams did un - rav -
E♭sus
Fm11
E♭/G
- el before I be - lieved in a hope that was
D♭6/9
D♭maj9
Fm11
E♭/G
true? And how long, how far?
What was meant
What was meant

G♭6/9(no3rd)
D♭sus2
B♭m7♭5/E
to ful-fill on-ly emp - tied me still,
to il-lu - mi-nate shad - owed me still,
and all You ev - er want - ed:
Fm7
D♭maj9
A♭sus2
on - ly me on my knees sing - ing, "Ho - ly, ho -
E♭/G
Fm
D♭maj9
- ly." And some - how all that mat - ters now is, You are ho -
A♭sus2
To Coda
E♭/G
- ly, ho - ly.
Da da da

85

E♭sus
6fr
A♭(add2)
4fr
wit - ness to 'til the proof was dis - proved in the
D♭maj9
3fr
D.S. al Coda
end? And how
CODA
E♭/G
3fr
- ly.
G♭(add2)
6fr
D♭/F
B♭m7♭5/E
And all I have is grat - i - tude to of -
Fm7
- fer You.
(Da da da da da da

87

88

Lyrics:

Some-how all that matters now is, You are ho-ly,
da da da da ya ya ya, ho-ly.
(You are ho-ly.)

Ho-ly, ho-ly-y, ho-ly.

I BELIEVE

Words and Music by
ALISA GIRARD

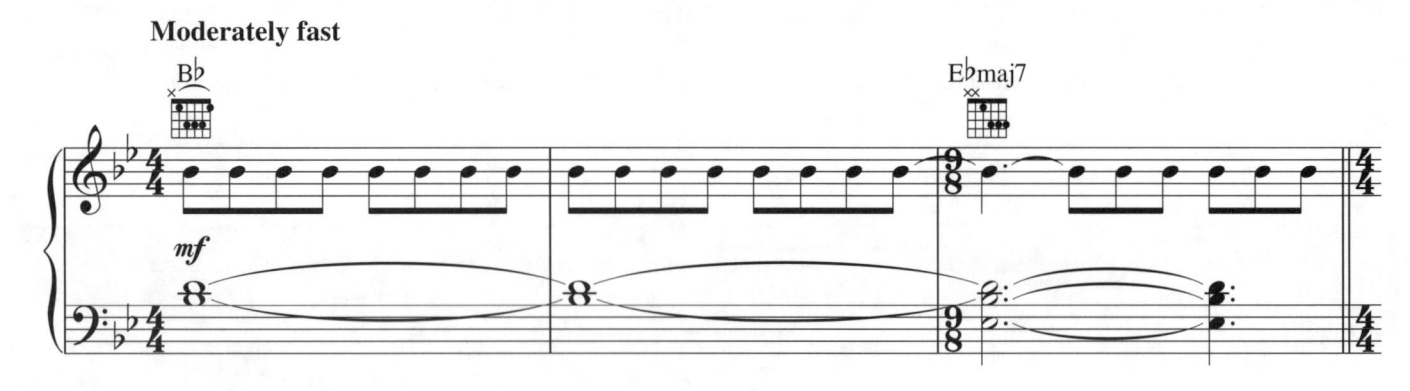

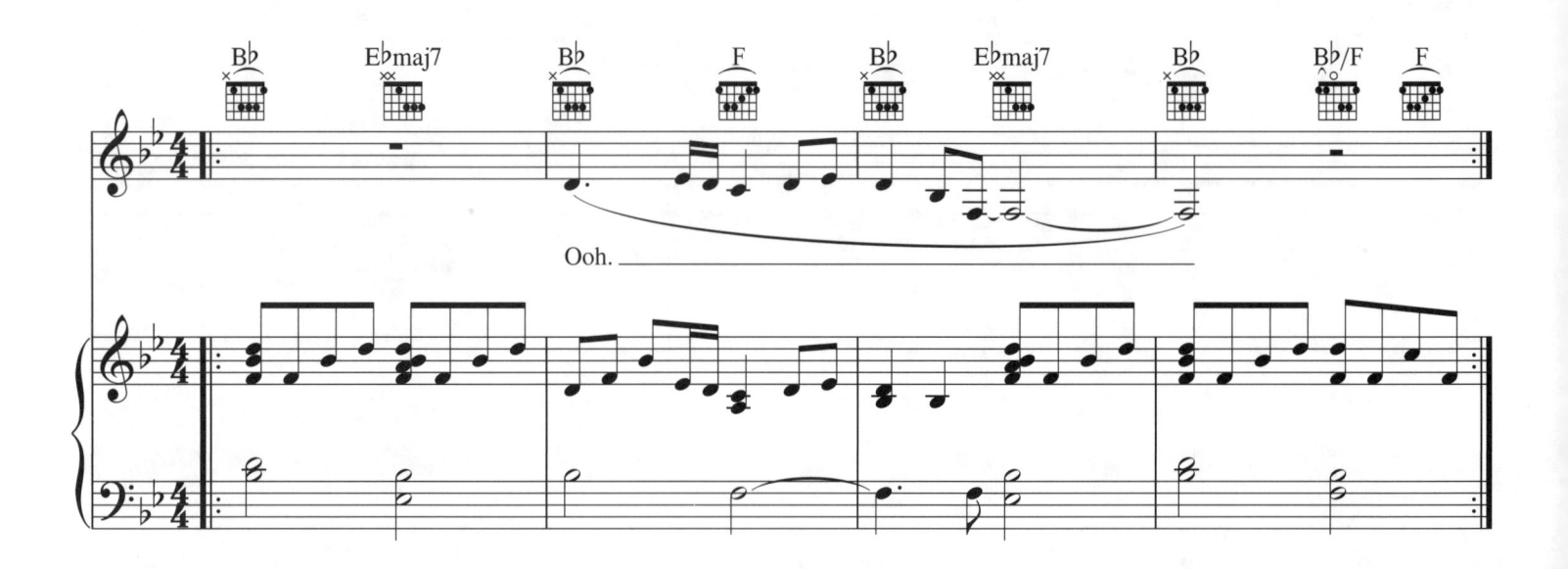

Moderately fast

I used to close my eyes and pray the time would pass me by so I could fly a-way in my dreams

Original key: B major. This edition has been transposed down one-half step in order to be more playable.

© 2000 BIRDWING MUSIC
Admin. by EMI CHRISTIAN MUSIC PUBLISHING
All Rights Reserved   Used by Permission

to an-y-where un-real, and I'd hide a-way from ev-'ry-thing.

I did-n't know what was real; I did-n't know the truth.
Now at the end of day when noth-ing seems to go my way

There was a day when some-bod-y in-tro-duced me to You, and You breathed
I've got a friend, I've got a love that's nev-er gon-na let me go, since You gave

B♭
Fm7
Your life in me.
Your life to me.
(You
Fsus
F
B♭
set me free.)
Now I'll shout
B♭/D
Cm9
D/F♯
it from the moun - tain that I'm not the same that I
Gm
Cm7
E♭
used to be. I be - lieve in God, be - lieve in God.

I'm not a-shamed to talk about it to a world that slow-ly slips a-way, that I be-lieve in God, be-lieve in God. (I be-lieve in God.)

Oh, when I feel so a - lone,
Oh, when my e - mo - tions flow,

He comes to sweet-ly say, "It's all gon-na be o-kay." Now I'll shout it from the moun-tain. Now I'll shout it from the moun-tain.

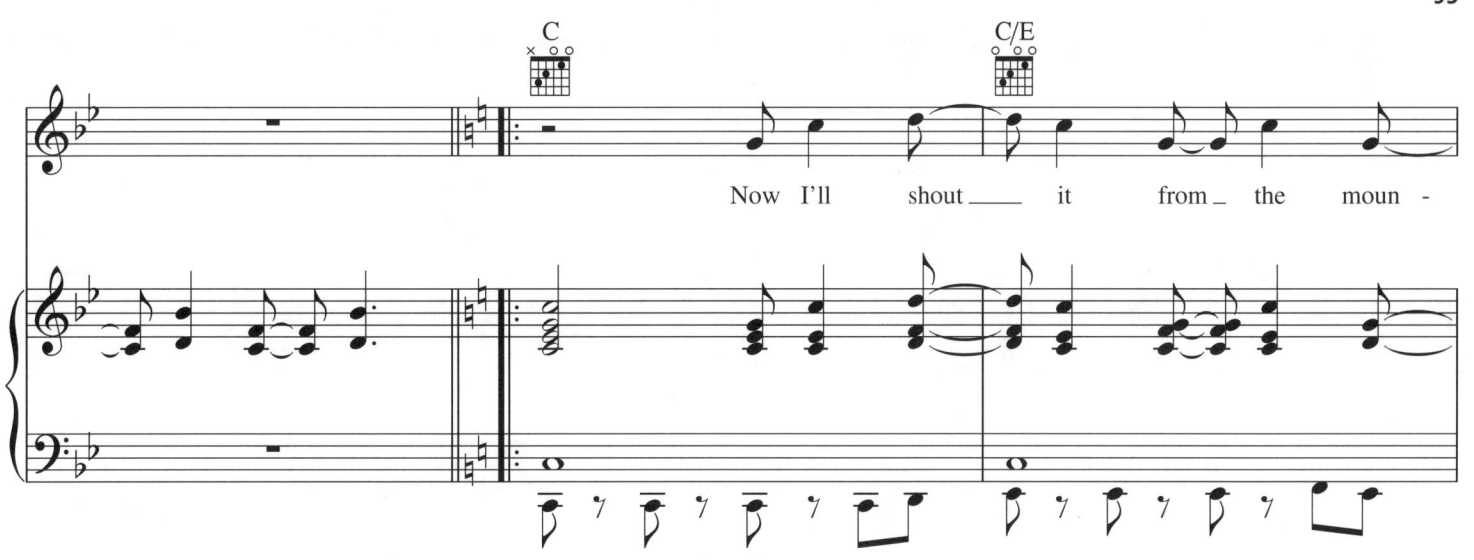

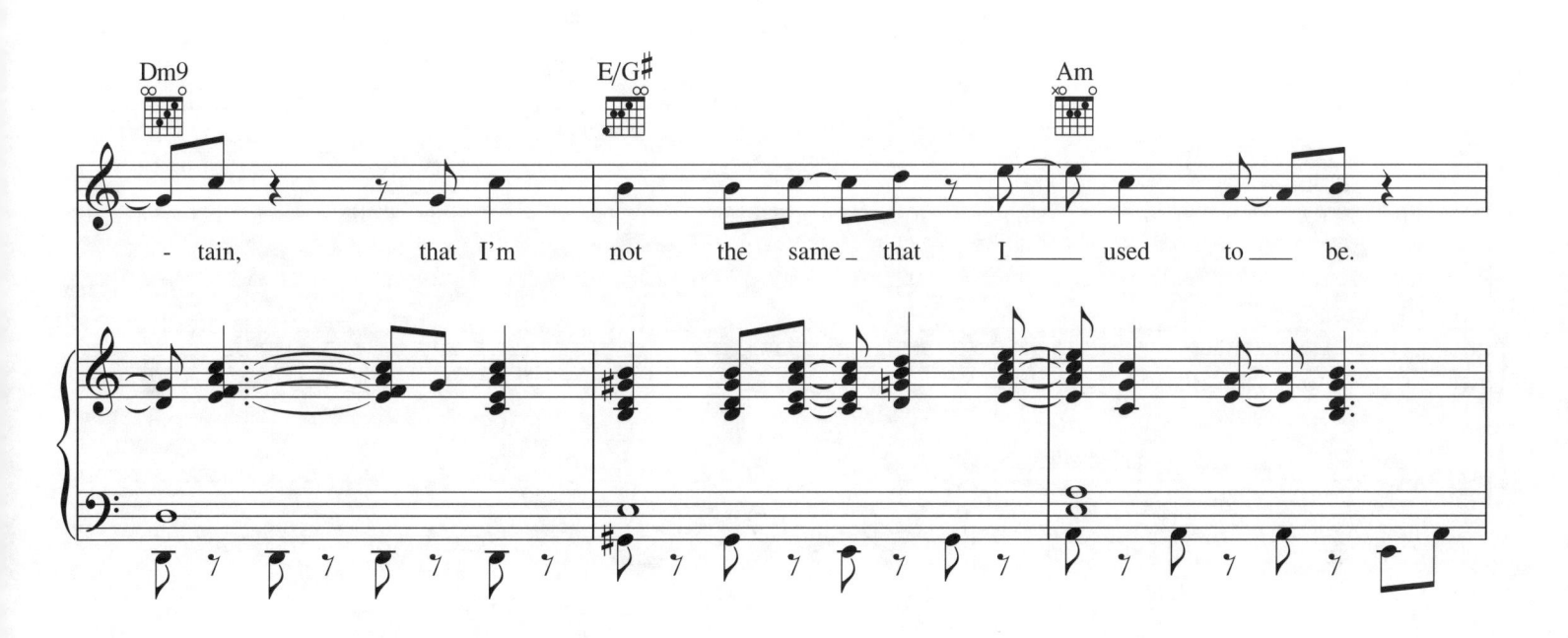

Now I'll shout it from the mountain, that I'm not the same that I used to be. I believe in God, believe in God. (I believe in God.)

Lyrics:

I'm not afraid to talk about it to a world that slowly slips away, that I believe in God, believe in God.

(I believe in God.)

IF YOU WANT ME TO

Words and Music by GINNY OWENS
and KYLE MATTHEWS

Reflectively ♩ = 63

with much freedom throughout

1. The pathway is broken and the signs are unclear. And I don't know the reason

Copyright © 1999 by BMG Songs, Inc. and Above The Rim Music
All Rights Administered by BMG Songs, Inc.
International Copyright Secured   All Rights Reserved

why You brought me here. But just be-cause You love me the way that You do, I'm gon-na walk through the val-ley if You want me to.

2. No, I'm

not who I was when I took my first step.

And I'm clingin' to the prom - ise You're not

through with me yet. So if all of these tri -

als bring me clos - er to You, then I will

go through the fi - re if You_____ want_____ me to._____

It may not be_____ the way_____ I_____ would have chos - en,_____ when You lead me through_____ a world_____

_____ that's not my home.

But You nev-er said_____ it would_____ be eas - y,

You on - ly said_____ I'll nev-er go a - lone.

3. So when the whole world turns a-gainst me and I'm all by— my-self— and I can't hear— You an-

-swer my cries for help, I'll re-member the suff'ring that Your love put You through. And I will walk through the darkness if You want me to. 4. 'Cause when I cross over Jor-

-dan I'm gonna sing, gonna shout. I'm gonna look into Your eyes and see You never let me down. So take me on the pathway that leads me home to You, and I will walk through the valley___ if You want___ me to.

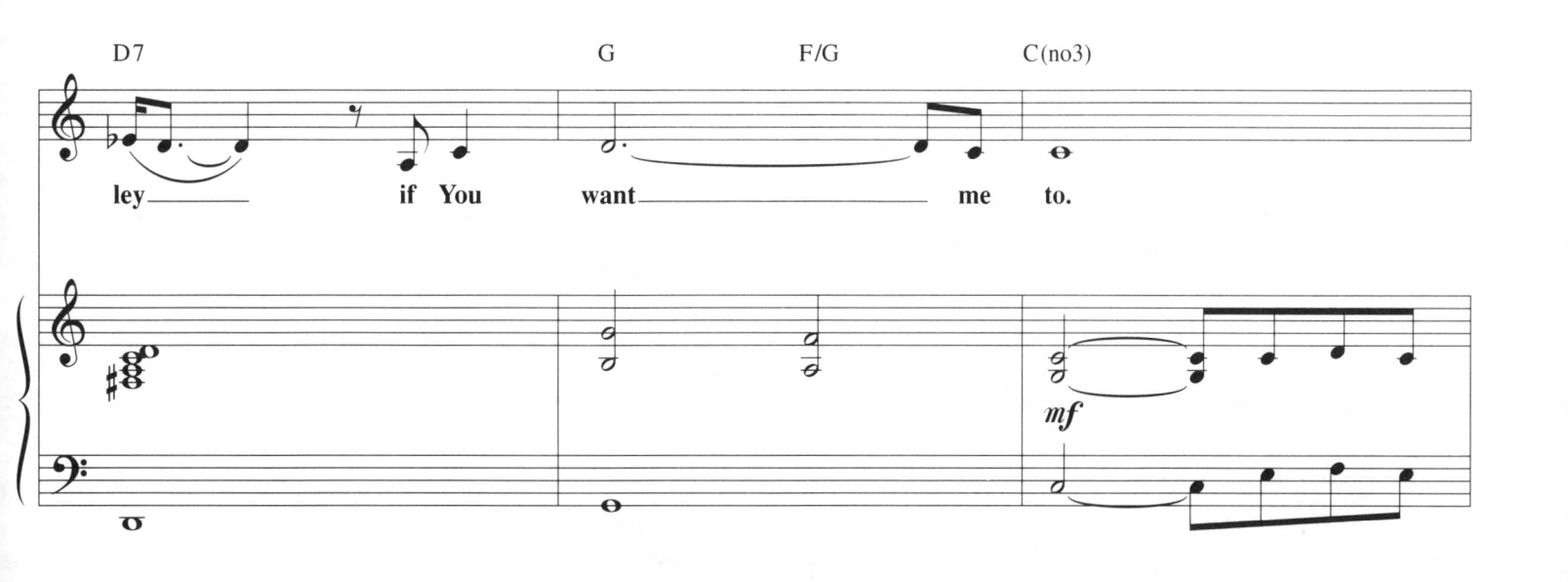

Yes, I will walk through the val - ley___ if You___ want___ me to.

I CAN ONLY IMAGINE

Reflectively

Words and Music by
BART MILLARD

I can only imagine what it will be like when I walk by Your side. I can only i-

Copyright © 2002 Simpleville Music
All Rights Administered by Fun Attic Music
All Rights Reserved Used by Permission

Emaj9
mag - ine what my eyes will see when Your face
Amaj9
Emaj9
is be - fore me. I can on - ly i - mag - ine.
Amaj9
Sur
Asus2
B(add4)
round - ed by Your glo - ry, what will my heart feel? Will I dance
mf

E(add2)
E
Emaj7
for You, Je - sus, or in awe of You be still? Will I stand
Asus2
B(add4)
in Your pres - ence or to my knees will I fall? Will I sing
E(add2)
E
Emaj7
hal - le - lu - jah? Will I be a - ble to speak at all? I can on - ly
To Coda
Asus2
B(add4)
i - mag - ine, I can on - ly i - mag -

Emaj7
- ine. I can on - ly i - mag - ine when that day
comes and I find my - self
Amaj9
stand - ing in
B7sus
the Son. I can on - ly i - mag - ine
Emaj7
when all I
will do is for - ev -
Amaj9
er, for - ev - er wor -

B7sus
2fr
Emaj7
- ship You.
I can on - ly i - mag - ine,
Amaj9
B7sus
2fr
D.S. al Coda
I can on - ly i - mag - ine.
Sur-
CODA
B(add4)
E
I can on - ly i - mag - ine.
Asus2
Sur - round - ed by Your glo - ry, what
f

will my heart feel? Will I dance for You, Jesus, or in awe of You be still? Will I stand in Your presence or to my knees will I fall? Will I sing hallelujah? Will I be able to speak at all? I can only imagine, yeah,

Bsus
Emaj7
E
I can on - ly i - mag - ine.
Emaj7
E
Asus2
I can on - ly i - mag - ine, yeah,
Bsus
Emaj7
E
I can on - ly i - mag - ine.
Emaj7
E
Asus2
I can on - ly i - mag - ine,

Bsus
C♯m9
I can on - ly i - mag - ine.
Amaj7
B(add4)
I can on - ly i - mag - ine when all I will do is for - ev -
mp
G♯m/C♯
C♯m
4fr
4fr
E
- er, for - ev - er wor - ship You.
Amaj9
B
E
I can on - ly i - mag - ine.

IF THIS WORLD

Words and Music by MICHELLE TUMES,
TYLER HAYES, ERIK SUNDIN
and MARK HEIMERMANN

Happily ♩ = 104

1. Do you feel you've been dis-owned, left out-side in the cold and with-out a home? Do you think that no one cares that you're lost and a-lone and with-out a prayer?

2. Are you look-ing for a friend who will stand by your side to the ver-y end? Some-one who is al-ways true to his word, be as-sured He won't turn from you.

116

Em7   **D/F#**

Don't give in____ to the lie____ that there's no
Put your faith____ in the One____ Who will nev-

Asus   **A**   **Bm**

__ one____ you____ can turn____ to.____
-er____ let____ you down.____

Em7   **D/F#**

Don't lose heart,____ there is hope,____ there is some-
He has prov-en His love.____ O - pen up____

Asus   **A**

-one who will nev - er de-sert____ you, oh.____
to all He has for you now,____ oh.____

If this world is a lone-ly place for you, fall in-to the arms of love.

If this world is a lone-ly place for you,

2nd time to CODA

there's a God who you can trust, who'll com-fort you and lift you up.

118

Na, na, na, na, na, na, na, na, na, na, na.

Oh, yeah. Na, na, na, na, na, na, na,

D.S. al CODA

na, na, na, na, na. Oh, yeah.

CODA

He hears your cry, He sees your

tears, He knows your pain and all your fears.

He waits for you with o-pen arms,

He longs to live in-side your heart.

You'll nev-er be a-lone a-gain.

D A Bm
If this world is a lone - ly place for you,
G A D
fall in - to the arms of love. If this world
A Bm
is a lone - ly place for you,
G A Bm A/C♯
there's a God who you can trust, who'll com - fort you and lift you up.

Na, na, na, na, na, na, na, na, na, na, na.

Oh, yeah. Na, na, na, na, na, na, na, na, na, na, na, na.

Oh, yeah. Na, na, na, na, na, na, na,

na, na, na, na, na. Oh, yeah.

JUST ONE

Words and Music by CONNIE HARRINGTON
and JIM COOPER

Free-Spirited Rock

As we change as a man, and the answers are a dime a dozen, points of view are like sand stretch-in' out

much at stake to be wast-ing time on im-i-ta-tions, prom-i-ses (prom-i-ses) and claims. There will nev-

Copyright © 1997 Lehsem Music, LLC and Lehsem Songs
Administered by Music & Media International, Inc.
International Copyright Secured   All Rights Reserved

___ as far ___ as the eye ___ can see. There's a thou-
-er be ___ a ___ sub - sti - tute for the blood, ___

___ sand dif - f'rent phi - los - o - phies, but there's just ___
___ the Word, ___ and the sim - ple truth, 'cause there's just ___

(Harmony both times)

___ one book, ___ and there's just ___ one name with the pow-
___ one book, ___ and there's just ___ one name with the pow-

-er to you ___ and the grace ___ to ___ save. You can search ___
-er to you ___ and the grace ___ to ___ save. You can search ___

the world for another way, but if you're
the world for another way, but if you're

lookin' for the road to beyond, there's just one. There's just too
lookin for the road to beyond,

Lead vocal:
there's just one door to open, where truth and hope will be wait-

(Background vocals:)
(door)

-ing there on the other side. Just one story that's nev-
(on the other side)

-er ending with life beginning in Jesus Christ,

yeah.

(Harmony each time)
F
You can search the world for an - oth -
B♭
A♭maj7
- er way, but if you're look - in' for the road to be - yond,
B♭
F
there's just one, just one book, and there's just
B♭
F
A♭
4 fr
Repeat and Fade
one name with the pow - er to heal and the grace to save. You can search

LIVE OUT LOUD

Words and Music by STEVEN CURTIS CHAPMAN
and GEOFF MOORE

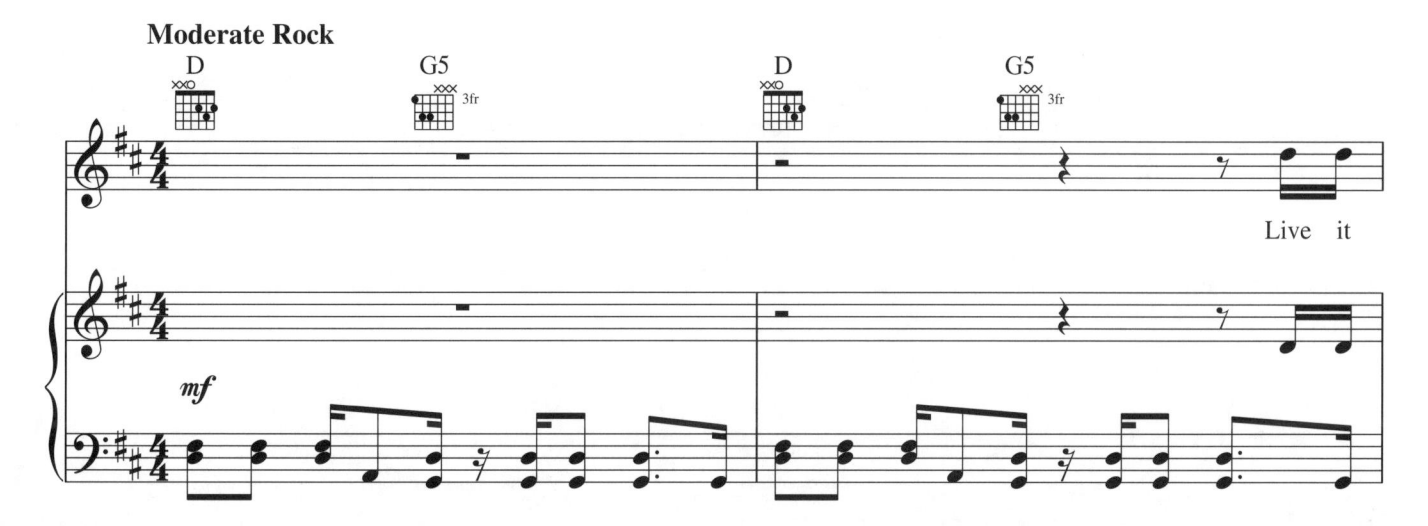

Moderate Rock

Live it out. Live it out, live it out. Oh, oh, yeah! Here we

Original key: D♭ major. This edition has been transposed up one half-step to be more playable.

© 2001 SPARROW SONG, PEACH HILL SONGS, SONGS ON THE FOREFRONT and GEOFF MOORE SONGS
Admin. by EMI CHRISTIAN MUSIC PUBLISHING
All Rights Reserved   Used by Permission

go.

I - mag - ine

this: I get a phone call from Re - gis. He says, "Do you want to be a mil - lion - aire?"
this: Try to keep a bird from sing - ing af - ter it's soared up in the sky;

They put me on the show and I win with two life - lines to spare. Now pic - ture
give the sun a cloud - less day and tell it not to shine. Now think a - bout

this: I act like noth - ing ev - er hap - pened and bur - y all the mon - ey in a cof - fee can.
this: If we real - ly have been giv - en the gift of a life that will nev - er end,

Bm
A/C♯
D
D/F♯
G6/9
Well, I've been giv - en more than Re - gis ev - er gave a - way.
and if we have been filled with liv - ing hope, we're gon - na o - ver-flow,
Bm
A/C♯
D
D/F♯
G6/9
I was a dead man who was called to come out of my grave.
and if God's love is burn - ing in our hearts we're gon - na glow.
Bm
A/C♯
Gsus2
And I think it's time for mak - in' some noise.
There's just no way to keep it in.
Wake the
D
G
D
G
neigh - bors; get the word out. Come on,
f

D
G
Bm7
A/C♯
crank up the mu - sic, climb a moun - tain and shout. __ This is
D
G
Bm
Bm/A
life we've been giv - en, made to be lived out, __ so
1
G
C
C♯dim
4fr
D
G(add2)
la la la la, live __ out loud. __ Yeah. __
D
G(add2)
D
G(add2)
Live __ out loud, yeah.

D G(add2) 2 G A7 B♭dim7 Bm
Think a - bout la la la la, live out loud.
B♭m Am G Am B♭m Bm B♭m Am G Am B♭m
Live out
Bm B♭m Am G C5 C♯5 D5
3fr 4fr 5fr
loud. Ev - 'ry - bod -
Bm B♭m Am G Am B♭m Bm B♭m Am G Am B♭m
- y, come on.
(La la la, la la la la,

132

Lyrics:

Ev-'ry corner of cre-a-tion is a liv-ing de-cla-ra-tion. Come join the song we were made to sing. Wake the neigh-bors; get the word out. Come on crank up the mu-sic, climb a moun-tain and shout. This is life we've been giv-en, made to be lived out, so la la la la, live out loud.

(Wake the neighbors, get the word out.) Get the word out. Come on, crank up the music, climb a mountain and shout. This is life we've been given, made to be lived out, so

A D D#dim E A(add2)
6fr
la la la la, live out loud. (La la la,
E A(add2) E A(add2) E A(add2)
la la la la, la la la, live out loud.)
E A(add2) E A(add2)
Wake the neigh - bors, get the word out.
(La la la, la la la la,
Repeat and Fade
Optional Ending
E A(add2) E A(add2) C#m7 E
4fr
la la la, live out loud.) live out loud.)

A LITTLE MORE

Words and Music by
JENNIFER KNAPP

Moderately

Turn Your eyes from on this way.
For all the sin that lives in me,

I have proved to live a dastardly day. I
it took a nail to set me free. Still,

hid my face from the saints and the an-
what I do I don't wanna do

© 2000 GOTEE MUSIC and WEST HUDSON MUSIC
Admin. by EMI CHRISTIAN MUSIC PUBLISHING
All Rights Reserved Used by Permission

Amaj7
E5
Amaj9
- gels who sing ___ of Your glo - ry. What You had in __
___ and ___ so ___ goes the sto - ry. What You had in __
E
Amaj9
___ mind, ___ said - a, ooh, ___ my weak -
___ mind, ___ said - a, when ___ we seek
E
Amaj9
ness shines.
we'll find.
Shine, ___ show me grace. A lit - tle more _ than I can give,
E/G#
E/F#
E
B
lit - tle more _ than I ___ de - serve, _ un - earth ___ this ho -

Amaj9
li - ness I can't earn. It's a lit - tle more _ than I can give,
E/G#
E/F#
E
1
B
lit - tle more _ than I ___ de - serve, ___
Amaj9
2
B
Bsus
2fr
oh.
yeah, _
Amaj7
ah, ___ dah. ___
With all this mo - ti - va - tion, I _

still find a hesitation deep in my soul.

Oh, and despite all my demanding, I still find You understanding. Show me grace, show me grace

I know is

a, oh, it's a little more than I can give, a little more than I deserve, unearth this holiness I can't earn. It's a little more than I can give,

lit - tle more than I de - serve,

yeah. yeah.

MAGNIFICENT OBSESSION

Words and Music by
STEVEN CURTIS CHAPMAN

Lord, You know how much

© 2001 SPARROW SONG and PEACH HILL SONGS
Admin. by EMI CHRISTIAN MUSIC PUBLISHING
All Rights Reserved   Used by Permission

I want to know so much in the way of answers and ex-pla-na-tions. I have cried and prayed, and still I seem to stay in the mid-dle of life's com-pli-ca-tions. All this pur-su-ing leaves me

144

| D♭6/9 | B♭maj7 |

feel-ing like I'm chas-ing down the wind, but now it's brought me back to You

| B♭sus | E♭ | B♭ |

and I can see a-gain. This is ev-'ry-thing I want.

cresc.   *mf*

| Cm7 | A♭(add9) | E♭ | B♭ |

This is ev-'ry-thing I need. I want this to be my one con-

| Cm | B♭ | A♭(add9) | E♭ | B♭(add4) |

sum-ing pas-sion. Ev-'ry-thing my heart de-sires,

145

Lord, I want it all to be for You, Jesus.

Be my mag-nif-i-cent ob-ses-sion.

Yeah.

So cap-ture my heart a-gain.

146

B♭sus/D | **Cm**

Take me to depths I've nev-er been, in-to the rich-es of Your

A♭(add9) | **B♭sus** **E♭**

grace and Your mer-cy. Re-turn me to the cross

B♭sus/D | **Cm7**

and let me be com-plete-ly lost in the won-der of the love

A♭(add9) | **B♭7** **Bmaj7**

that You've shown me. Cut through these chains that tie me down

D♭6/9
Bmaj7
to so man - y less - er things. Let all my dreams fall to the ground
B♭sus
E♭
B♭(add4)
un - til this one re - mains. This is ev - 'ry - thing I want.
Cm7
A♭(add9)
E♭
B♭(add4)
This is ev - 'ry - thing I need. I want this to be my one con -
B♭
Cm
B♭
A♭(add9)
E♭
B♭(add4)
sum - ing pas - sion. Ev - 'ry - thing my heart de - sires,

Lord, I want it all to be for You, Jesus.

Be my mag-nif-i-cent ob-ses-sion.

My mag-nif-i-cent ob-ses-sion.

Yeah, yeah, yeah, yeah.

Lyrics:

You are ev-'ry-thing I want, and You are ev-'ry-thing I need. Lord, You are all my heart desires. You are ev-'ry-thing to me. You are ev-'ry-thing I want.

150

You are ev-'ry-thing I need. I want You to be my one con-suming pas-sion. Ev-'ry-thing my heart de-sires, Lord, I want it all to be for You, I want it all to be for You. 'Cause You are ev-'ry-thing I want.

| Cm7 | A♭(add9) | E♭ | B♭(add4) |

You are ev-'ry-thing I need. I want You to be my one con-

| B♭ | Cm | B♭ | A♭(add9) | E♭ | B♭(add4) |

sum-ing pas-sion. Ev-'ry-thing my heart de-sires,

| Cm7 | A♭(add9) | Cm7 |

Lord, I want it all to be for You, Je-sus.

| Bmaj7 | D♭ | Bmaj7 |

Be my mag-nif-i-cent ob-ses- sion.

Be my mag-nif-i-cent ob-ses - sion.

Hey, yeah, yeah.

153

MERCY CAME RUNNING

*Words and Music by DAN DEAN,
DAVE CLARK and DON KOCH*

Flowing

Once there was a ho-ly place,
Once there was a bro-ken heart,

ev-i-dence of God's em-brace;
way too hu-man from the start;

© 1995, 1996 DAWN TREADER MUSIC, DUDEDABE MUSIC, WORD MUSIC, INC., DAYSPRING MUSIC, INC., DEFINITIVE MUSIC and FIRST VERSE MUSIC
DAWN TREADER MUSIC and DUDEDABE MUSIC Admin. by EMI CHRISTIAN MUSIC PUBLISHING
DEFINITIVE MUSIC Admin. by DAYSPRING MUSIC, INC.
All Rights Reserved   Used by Permission

and I can al - most see mer - cy's face
And all the years left it torn a - part,

pressed a - gainst the veil.
hope - less and a - fraid.

Look - ing down with long - ing eyes
Walls I nev - er meant to build

mer - cy must have re - al - ized
left this pris - 'ner un - ful - filled.

that once His blood was sac - ri - ficed
Free - dom called but e - ven_ still_ it

free - dom would_ pre - vail.__ And as the
seemed so far_ a - way.__ I was

sky grew_ dark_ and the earth be - gan_ to shake,_ with
bound by_ the chains_ from the wa - ges of_ my sin,_

jus - tice_ no long - er in the way._____
just when_ I felt like giv - in' in,_____ Mer - cy came_ a - run - nin'

like a pris-'ner set free, past all my fail-ures to the point of my need; when the sin that I car-ried was all I could see. And when I could not reach mer-cy, mer-cy came a-run-nin' to me.

Some - times I still feel so far, so far from where I real - ly should be. He gent - ly calls to my heart just to re - mind me: Mer - cy came a - run - nin'

like a pris-'ner set free, past all my fail-ures to the point of my need; when the sin that I car-ried was all I could see. And when I could not reach mer-cy, mer-cy came, mer-cy came a-run-nin'

Repeat and Fade

MY WILL

*Words and Music by TOBY McKEEHAN,
MICHAEL TAIT, JOEY ELWOOD and DANIEL PITTS*

Medium Rock Ballad

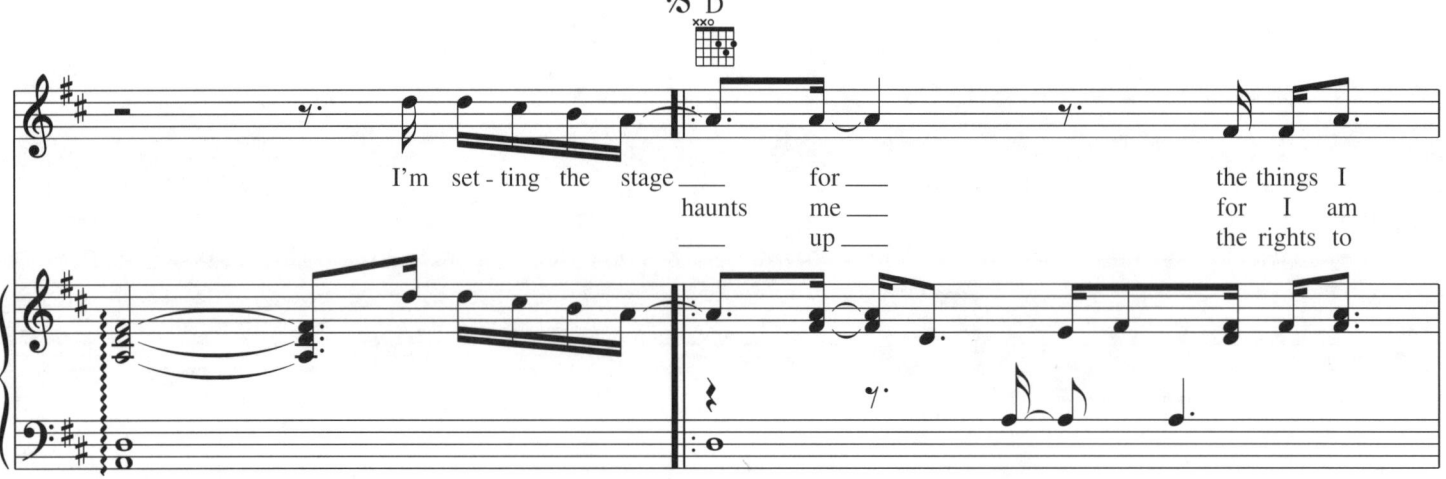

I'm set-ting the stage ___ for ___ the things I
haunts me ___ for I am
up ___ the rights to

love, ___ and I'm now the man ___ I ___ once could-n't
two men, en-trenched in a bat-tle ___ that I'll nev-er
my-self, ___ the bits and the piec-es ___ I've gath-ered as

© 1998 ACHTOBER SONGS, OUT OF TWISTED ROOTS, GOTEE MUSIC and PAINED MUSIC
ACHTOBER SONGS, OUT OF TWISTED ROOTS and GOTEE MUSIC Administered by EMI CHRISTIAN MUSIC PUBLISHING
All Rights Reserved   Used by Permission

A

be.
win.
wealth.

And noth-ing on earth could now ev-er
My dis-ci-pline fails me, my know-ledge it
They'd nev-er com-pare to the joy that You

D

Gmaj9

move me,
fools me,
bring me,

I now have the will and the strength a man
but You are my shel-ter, all the strength that
the peace that You show me is the strength that

D

A **D**

I needs.
I need.

It's my will, I'm not mov-

-ing, 'cause if it's Your will then noth-ing can shake me. And it's my will to bow and praise You, I now have the will to praise my God. Com-plex-i-ty

163

D
A
chil - dren of peace. Don't you know,
D
G
we've got to be
D
A
G
chil - dren of peace.
And it's my will,
D
G
I'm not mov - ing.
'Cause if it's Your
We've got to be

will, then nothing can shake me. And it's my will
children of peace.

We've got to bow and praise You, I now have the will
to be

to praise my God. It's my will
children of peace.

God.
It's Your will, it's Your will, not mine. It's Your will, it's Your will.

Em
G
C
It's Your will, it's Your will, not mine.
F
Em
3
G(add2)
It's Your will, it's Your will.
And it's my will God.
And don't you know
D
G(add2)
D
A(add4)
we've got to be chil - dren of peace.
Don't you know
D
G(add2)
D
A
G
we've got to be chil - dren of peace.

STEADY ON

Words and Music by GRANT CUNNINGHAM
and MATT HUESMANN

Kick-in' up dust, heav-en or bust, we're head-ed for the prom-ised land. Since the mo-
wan-na walk a while; we know that ev-'ry mile is bring-ing us clos-er home. We wan-

© 1998 RIVER OAKS MUSIC COMPANY and MATT HUESMANN MUSIC (ASCAP)/Administered by BUG MUSIC
RIVER OAKS MUSIC COMPANY Admin. by EMI CHRISTIAN MUSIC PUBLISHING
All Rights Reserved Used by Permission

-ment we be-lieved we've been ea-ger to leave, like a child tug-gin' Dad-dy's hand. May we
-na tell the sto-ry of sin-ners bound for glo-ry and turn to find we're not a-lone. When we

nev-er for-get that pa-tience is a vir-tue. Calm our
walk in Your light, the lost will see You bet-ter. As the

an-xious feet so faith-ful hands can serve You, Lord. We
nar-row road gets crowd-ed, Lord, won't You lead us stead-y on?

run on up a-head, we lag be-hind You. It's

hard to wait when heav-en's on our minds.

Teach our rest-less feet to walk be-side You, 'cause in our

hearts we're al-read-y gone. Will You

walk with us stead-y on? We

2
F
Dm7
E♭
3fr
Stead - y me when the road of faith gets
F
Dm7
E♭
3fr
rock - y, and read - y me for fears I can - not see.
B♭
Dm7
E♭
3fr
Lord, won't You let me be a wit - ness to Your
F
E♭
3fr
B♭
prom - ise? Won't You stead - y me? Oh, yeah. We

run on up a-head, we lag be-hind You. It's hard to wait when heav-en's on our minds. Teach our rest-less feet to walk be-side You, 'cause in our hearts we're al-read-y gone. We

run on up__ a-head,__ we lag be-hind You. It's
hard to wait__ when heav-en's on our minds.__
Teach our rest-less feet to walk__ be-side__ You,__ 'cause in our
hearts we're al-read-y gone.__ Will You

walk with us stead-y on? Stead-y on, stead-y on, stead-y on, oh. Stead-y on, stead-y on, stead-y on, oh. Stead-y on, stead-y on, stead-y on, oh. Stead-y on, stead-y on, stead-y on, oh. ooh.

NO YOU

Words and Music by SHAUNA BOLTON,
ERROL JOHNSON, CHRISSY CONWAY
and JOE PRIOLO

G
D/F#
Am7
The sun and the moon shine bright, but my eyes are all Yours now.
And when my heart seems so far a - way, in - to Your arms
Dsus
3fr
C(add2)
Dsus
3fr
Don't know how I'd live with - out You.
is where I wan - na stay. Try to find the words to tell You
C(add2)
D
Em
D
C(add2)
I don't re - mem - ber how it used to feel. Lord, I can't i - mag -
all the things my heart's been tell - ing me. I don't wan - na know how
G/B
Am7
D9sus
- ine if I had no You to hold me.
it feels to have no You to love me.

Where would I go with no You to run to, no You to hold me when I am afraid? Who would I be with no You beside me? I oughta know it by now: without You there's no me, oh, there's no me. Where would I go with no You to run

Am
Em
D
G
to, no You to hold me when I am a - fraid? Who would I be
D
Am7
C
D7
with no You be - side me? I ought - ta know it by now: with - out You,
G
D
Am
where would I go
Where would I go
with no You to run to, no You to hold
Em
D
G
D
me when I am a - fraid? Who would I be with no You be - side

me? I ough-ta know it by now: with-out You there's no me, oh, there's no me. Where would I go? With-out

You there's no me, _____ oh, ___ there's no me. _____

Repeat and Fade

Optional Ending

RUN TO YOU

Words and Music by
TWILA PARIS

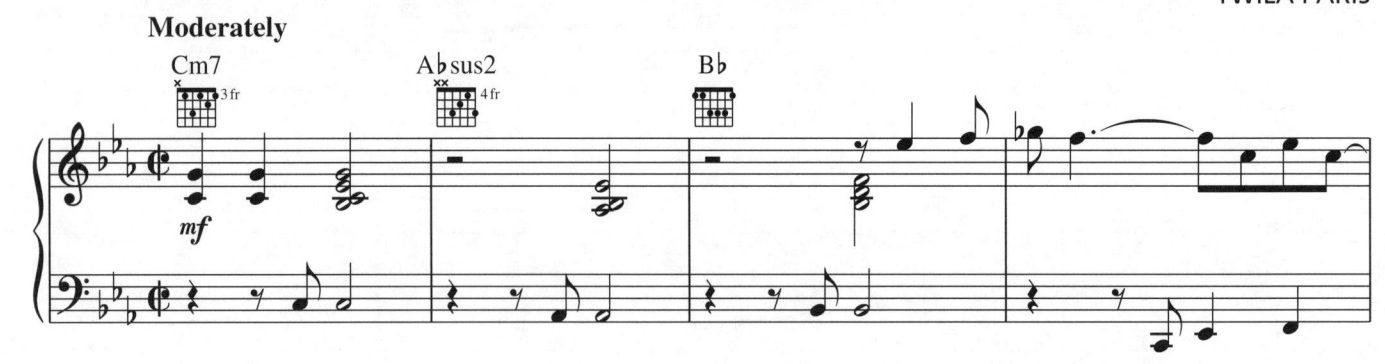

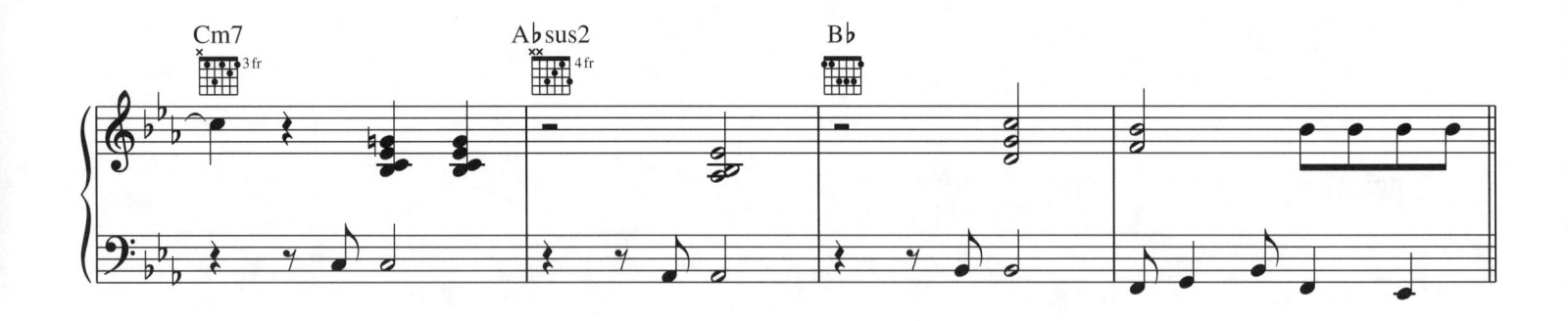

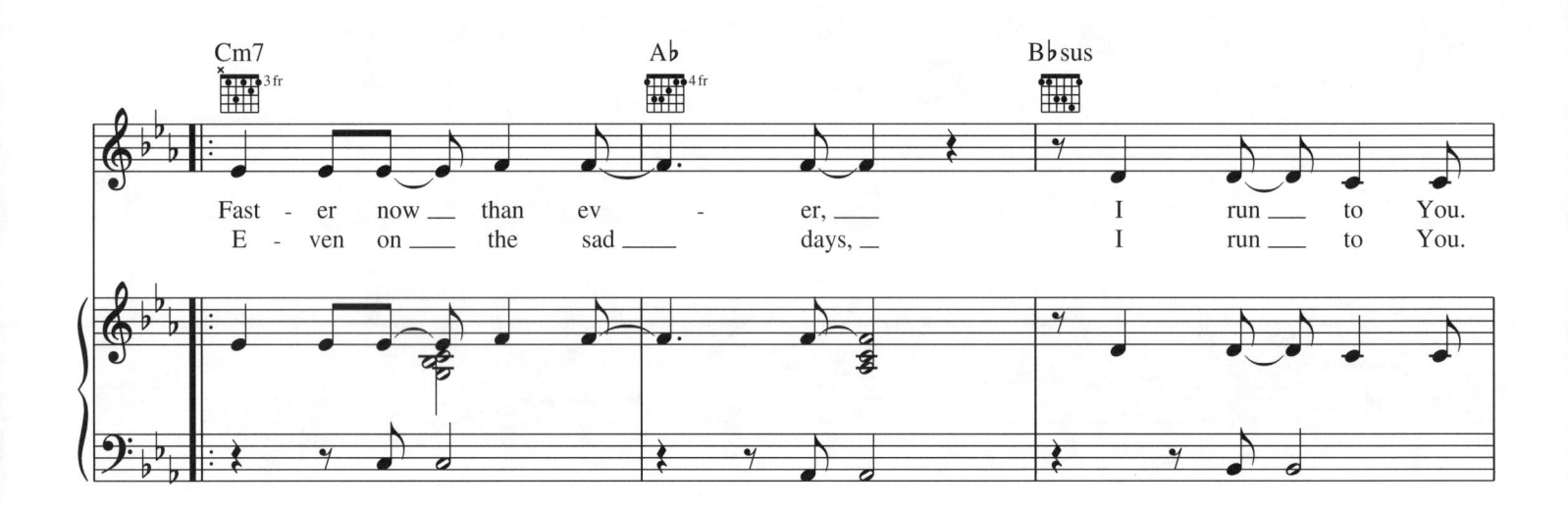

Faster now than ev - er, I run to You.
E - ven on the sad days, I run to You.

Now I know You bet - ter,
E - ven on the good days, too,

© 1999 ARIOSE MUSIC and MOUNTAIN SPRING MUSIC
Admin. by EMI CHRISTIAN MUSIC PUBLISHING
All Rights Reserved   Used by Permission

Bbsus
Cm7
3fr
I run to You.
I run to You.
I am a lit - tle old -
E - ven be - fore all
Ab
4fr
Bb
Eb/G
3fr
- er now,
else fails,
You know it's true.
You know it's true.
May -
You
Cm
3fr
Absus2
4fr
Bb
- be a lit - tle wis - er, too,
are the wind in my sails,
I run to You.
Eb/G
3fr
Ab
4fr
Bb
And I can see (I can see) deep -

-er than I did before. I do believe, (I believe)
never have I been so sure that I need
that I need
You ev-'ry min-ute, ev-'ry day,
You ev-'ry foot-step, all the way,
That I need You more than I could ev-er say.
That I need You so much more than I can say.

183

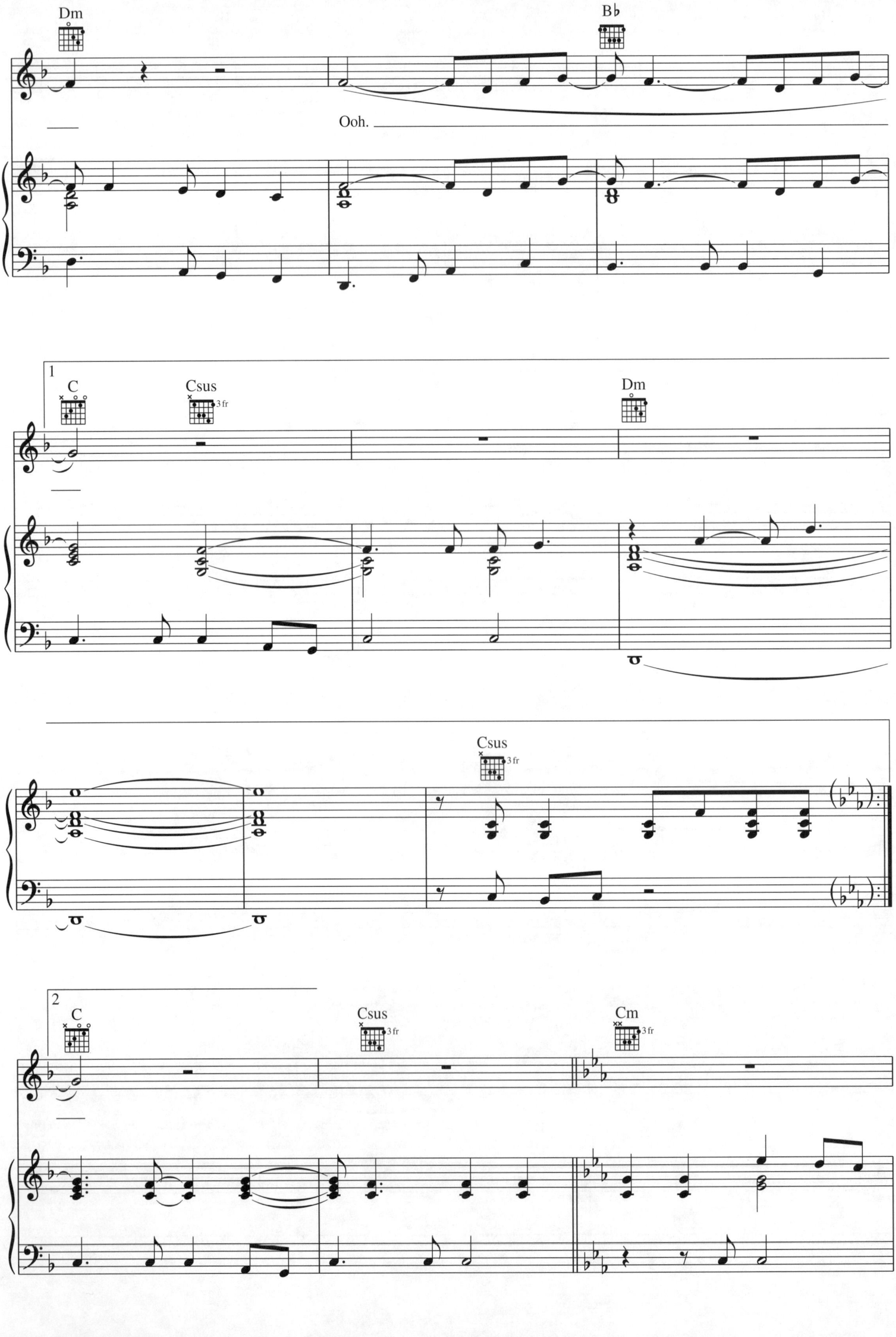
Dm
B♭
Ooh.
1
C
Csus
3 fr
Dm
Csus
3 fr
2
C
Csus
3 fr
Cm
3 fr

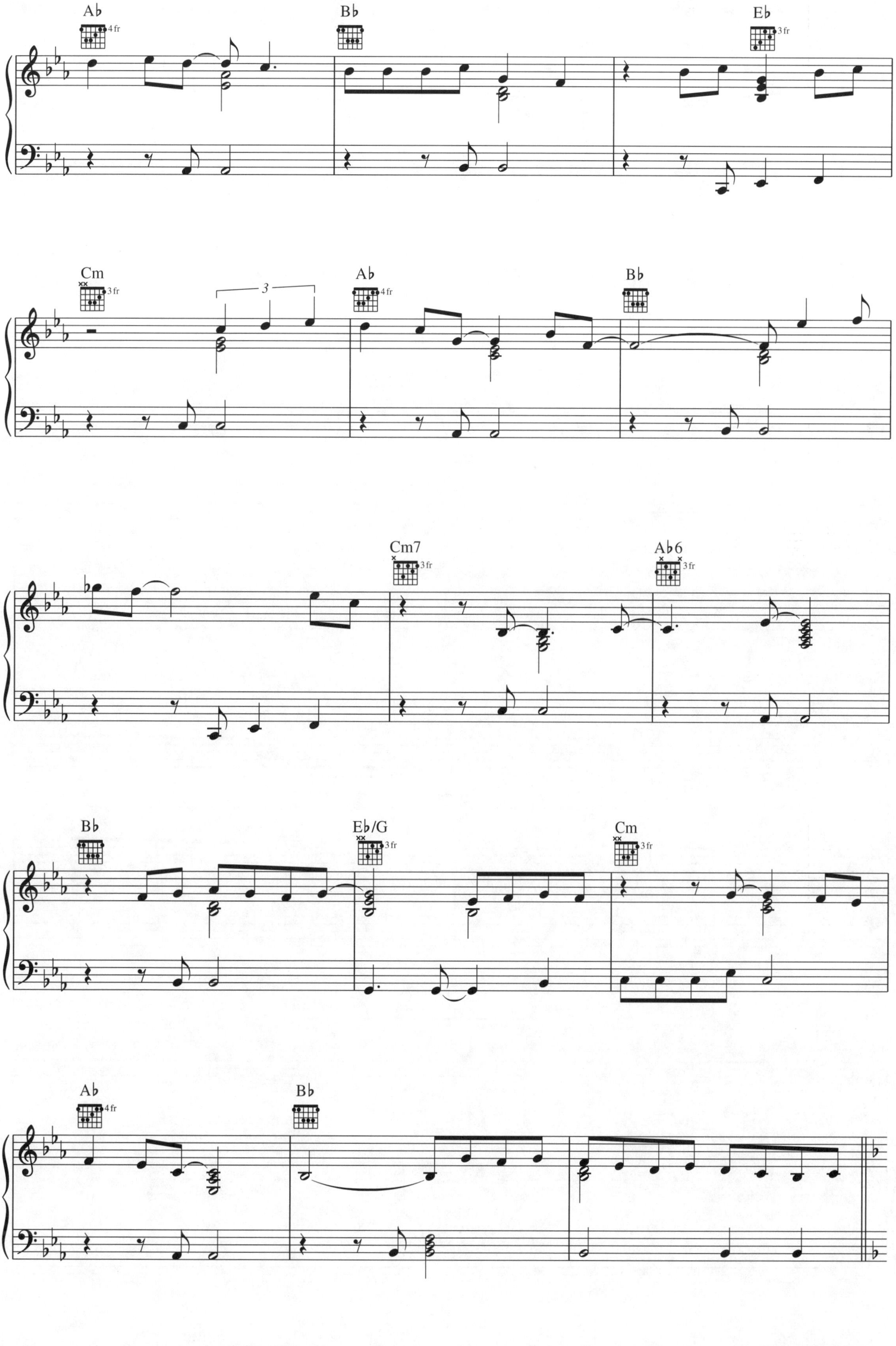
Ab
Bb
Eb
Cm
Ab
Bb
Cm7
Ab6
Bb
Eb/G
Cm
Ab
Bb

186

Dm
B♭
Ooh,
C
Dm
I run to You.
B♭
C
Ooh,
Optional Ending
Dm
Repeat and Fade
yeah, yeah.

SONG OF LOVE

*Words and Music by REBECCA ST. JAMES,
MATT BRONLEEWE and JEREMY ASH*

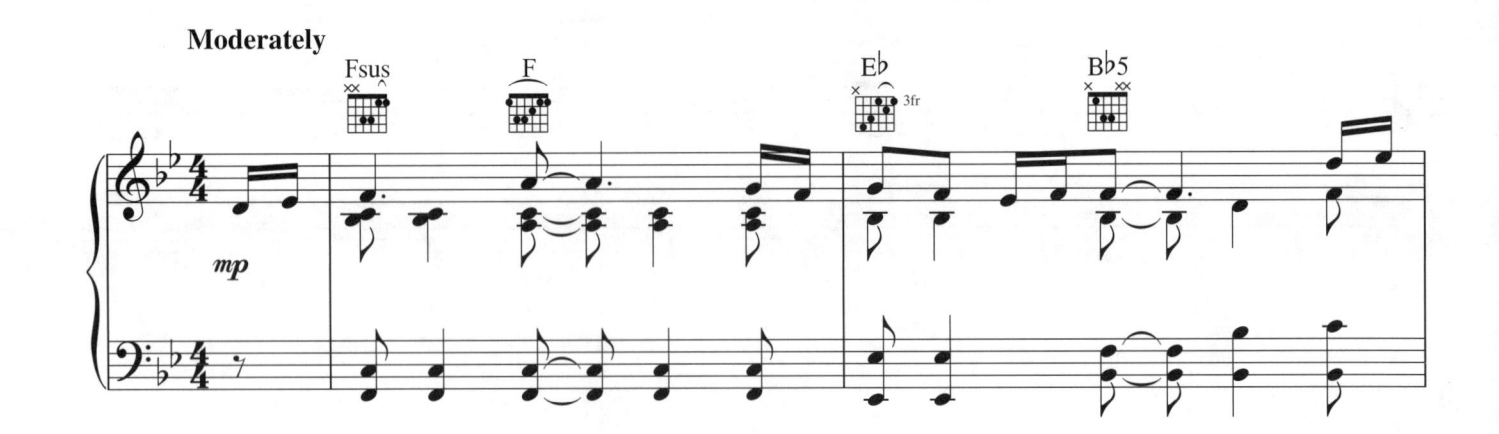

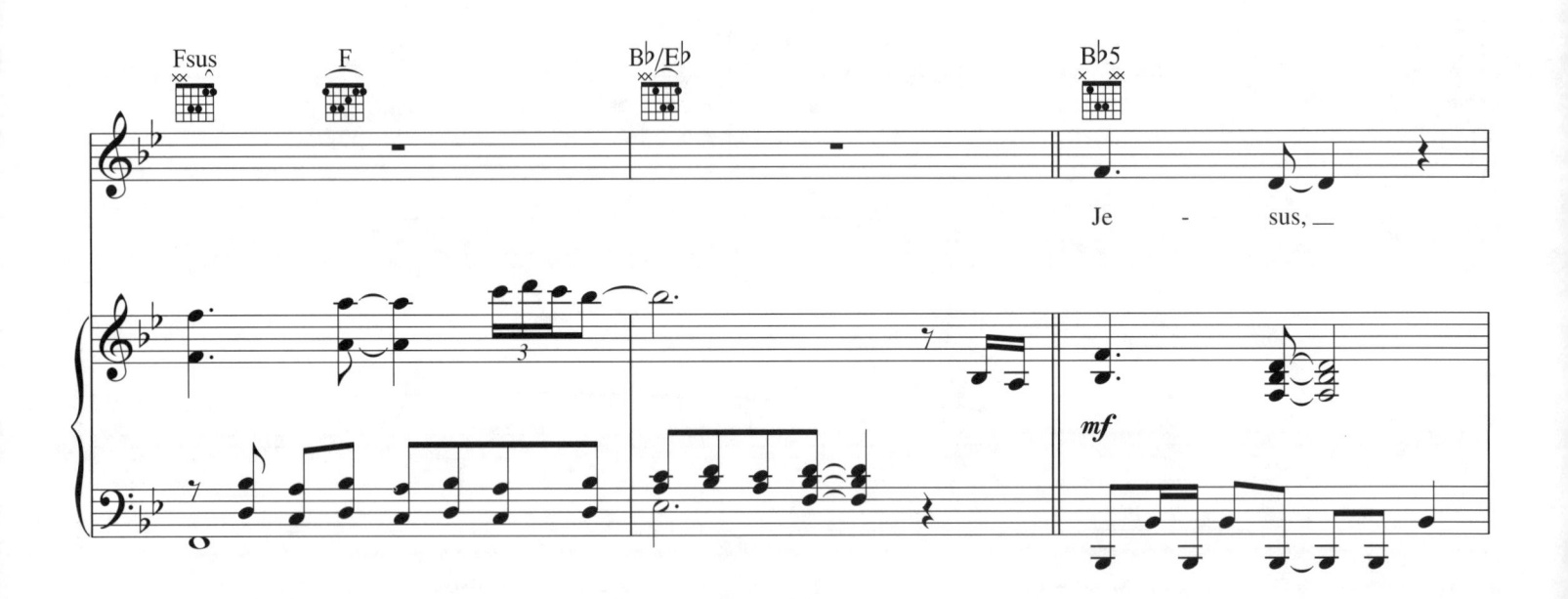

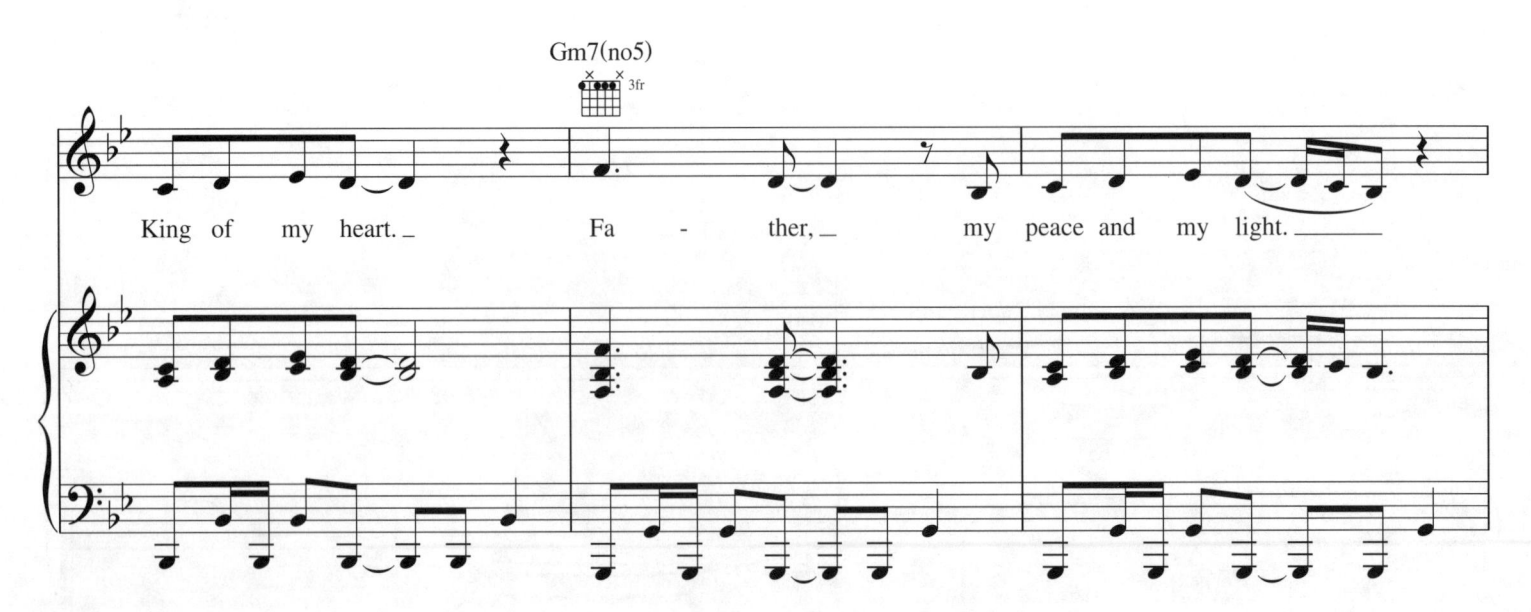

Moderately

Je- sus,___ King of my heart.___ Fa- ther,___ my peace and my light.___

Original key: B major. This edition has been transposed down one half-step to be more playable.

© 2002 UP IN THE MIX MUSIC, BIBBITSONG MUSIC, SONGS OF WINDSWEPT PACIFIC, SONGS FROM THE FARM and PROJECT 76
UP IN THE MIX MUSIC Admin. by EMI CHRISTIAN MUSIC PUBLISHING
BIBBITSONG MUSIC Admin. by ICG
All Rights Reserved   Used by Permission

Spirit, the joy of my soul You are.

Jesus, to You none compare.
Jesus, You saved my soul. I'll

Father, I rest in Your care. Spirit, the
thank You for-ev-er-more. Jesus, the

hope for my heart You are.
love of my life You are.

The

heav-ens ___ de-clare You are God, ___ and the moun-tains ___ re-joice. ___ The o-ceans ___ cry "Al-le-lu-ia" ___ as we wor-ship ___ You, Lord, ___ for

1.
this is our song __ of love. ___

Je - sus, I am in awe of the love that You have shown. Je - sus, how pre - cious You are to me, to me. The heav - ens de -

E♭ B♭ Fsus F
clare You are God, and the moun - tains re - joice.
E♭ B♭ Fsus F E♭ B♭
The o - ceans cry "Al - le - lu - ia" as we
1
Fsus/C B♭maj7/D
wor - ship You, Lord. The
2
Fsus/C B♭maj7/D E♭sus2
wor - ship You, Lord, as we

Fsus/C
B♭maj7/D
E♭sus2
wor - ship You, Lord, for this is our song of love.
dim.
B♭5
Gm7(no5)
mp
Our song of love,
E♭sus2
Repeat and Fade
F5
our song of love; this is our song of love.
B♭5
Optional Ending
F5
B♭5
this is our song of love.

TESTIFY TO LOVE

Words and Music by PAUL FIELD, HENK POOL,
RALPH VAN MANEN and ROBERT RIEKERK

All the col-ors of the rain - bow,_
From the moun-tains to the val - leys,_

© 1996, 1998 EMI MUSIC PUBLISHING LTD. and MCA MUSIC HOLLAND B.V.
All Rights for EMI MUSIC PUBLISHING LTD. in the U.S. and Canada Controlled and Administered by EMI LONGITUDE MUSIC
All Rights for MCA MUSIC HOLLAND B.V. in the Western Hemisphere Controlled and Administered by
UNIVERSAL - MCA MUSIC PUBLISHING, A Division of UNIVERSAL STUDIOS, INC.
All Rights Reserved   International Copyright Secured   Used by Permission

all the voices of the wind,
from the rivers to the sea,

ev - 'ry dream that reach - es out, _____ that
ev - 'ry hand that reach - es out, _____ ev - 'ry

reach - es out __ to find __ where love __ be - gins, _____
hand that reach - es out __ to of - fer peace, _____

ev - 'ry word __ of ev - 'ry sto - ry, _____
ev - 'ry sim - ple act _____ of mer - cy, _____

Cm
Bb
Ab
ev - 'ry star in ev - 'ry sky,
ev - 'ry step to king - dom come,
(Harmony 2nd time)
Fm7
Eb/G
Ab
Bb7sus
Bb7
Bb7sus
ev - 'ry cor - ner of cre - a - tion lives to tes - ti -
all the hope in ev - 'ry heart will speak what love has
Ab/Eb
Eb
fy.
done.
For as long as I shall
Bb
Cm
Cm/Bb
live, I will tes - ti - fy to love. I'll be a wit - ness in the si -

-lenc - es__ when words__ are not__ e - nough.___ With ev - 'ry breath__ I take, I will give thanks to God__ a - bove,___ for as long__ as I__ shall live, I will tes - ti - fy__ to love.___

live, I will tes - ti - fy__ to love. Tes - ti - fy,__ tes - ti - fy.__
Col - ors of the rain - bow, voic - es of the wind,

G♭
D♭/F
C♭maj7
Tes - ti - fy, tes - ti - fy.
dream that reach-es out where love be - gins,
word of ev - 'ry sto - ry, star in ev - 'ry sky,
1 B♭m7
D♭
E♭7
Tes - ti - fy, tes - ti - fy.
cor - ner of cre - a - tion tes - ti - fy.
Moun-tains to the val - leys, riv - ers to the sea,
G♭
C♭maj7
Tes - ti - fy, tes - ti - fy.
hand that reach-es out to of - fer peace, a
sim - ple act of mer - cy, king - dom come,
B♭m7
D♭
2 B♭m7
D♭
ev - 'ry heart will speak what love has done.
cor - ner of cre - a - tion tes - ti - fy.

E♭
B♭
For as long as I shall live, I'll
For as long as I shall live, I will tes - ti - fy to love.
Cm
Cm/B♭
A♭
A♭/B♭
Gm/B♭
tes - ti - fy, tes - ti - fy. All my life, I'll tes - ti - fy.
I'll be a wit - ness in the si - lenc - es when words are not e - nough.
E♭
B♭
Ev - 'ry breath I take, give thanks and
With ev - 'ry breath I take, I will give thanks to God a - bove,

200

For as long as I shall live, I'll testify to love. With ev-'ry breath I take, I will give thanks to God above, for as long as I shall live, I will testify to love. All my life, I'll testify. Ev-'ry breath I live, I will testify to love. Testify Your way,

C
Dm7
take, give thanks and tes - ti - fy, tes - ti - fy. All
tes - ti - fy Your truth, tes - ti - fy Your life, Your
Bb
Dm/C C
F
C
my life, I'll tes - ti - fy. For as long as I shall live, I'll
love and mer - cy. Tes - ti - fy Your way, tes - ti - fy Your truth,
Dm7
Bb
Dm/C C
F5
tes - ti - fy, tes - ti - fy. All my life, I'll tes - ti - fy.
tes - ti - fy Your life, Your love and mer - cy.

THIS IS YOUR TIME

Words and Music by MICHAEL W. SMITH
and WES KING

With conviction ♩. = 55

1. It was a test we could all hope to pass, but none of us would want to take.
2. Though you are mourning and grieving your loss, death died a long time ago.

Copyright © 1999 by Milene Music, Inc., Deer Valley Music, Sparrow Song and Uncle Ivan Music
All Rights for Deer Valley Music Administered by Milene Music, Inc.
All Rights for Sparrow Song and Uncle Ivan Music Administered by EMI Christian Music Publishing
All Rights Reserved   Used by Permission

Faced with the choice to de-ny God and live, for
Swal-lowed in life, so her life car-ries on,

her there was one choice to make.
still, it's so hard to let go.

This was her time, this was her dance, she lived ev-'ry mo-ment, left noth-in' to chance. She swam in the sea, drank of the deep, em-braced the mys-

2nd time to Coda

-ter-y of all____ she could be;____

This was her time.____

D.S. al CODA

CODA

-ter-y of all____ she____ could be. What if to-mor-

- row, and what if to - day faced with the ques -
B♭
F/A
- tion, oh, what would you say?
Gm7
E♭2
Cm7
B♭
Fsus/A
F/A
B♭
B♭/D
E♭2
f
Cm7
B♭
F/A
F
f
This is your time,

this is your dance, live ev-'ry mo - ment, leave noth-in' to chance. To swim in the sea, drink of the deep, and fall on the mer- cy and hear your-self pray - ing, "Won't You save me? Won't You save_____ me?"

ff

This is your time,___ this is your dance,___ live ev-'ry mo-

-ment, leave noth-in'___ to chance. Swim in the sea,___ drink of the deep,___

1.

___ em-brace the mys-ter-y___ of all you can be.___ This is your time,___

-ter-y of all___ you can be.___

ad lib. on repeat

This is your time.

Won't You save___

Repeat and fade

me?

TO KNOW YOU

Words and Music by NICHOLE NORDEMAN
and MARK HAMMOND

Moderately slow

It's well past midnight and I'm awake with questions that won't wait for daylight, separating fact from my imaginary fiction on this shelf of my conviction. I

© 1998 ARIOSE MUSIC and MARK HAMMOND MUSIC
ARIOSE MUSIC Admin. by EMI CHRISTIAN MUSIC PUBLISHING
MARK HAMMOND MUSIC Admin. by ICG
All Rights Reserved   Used by Permission

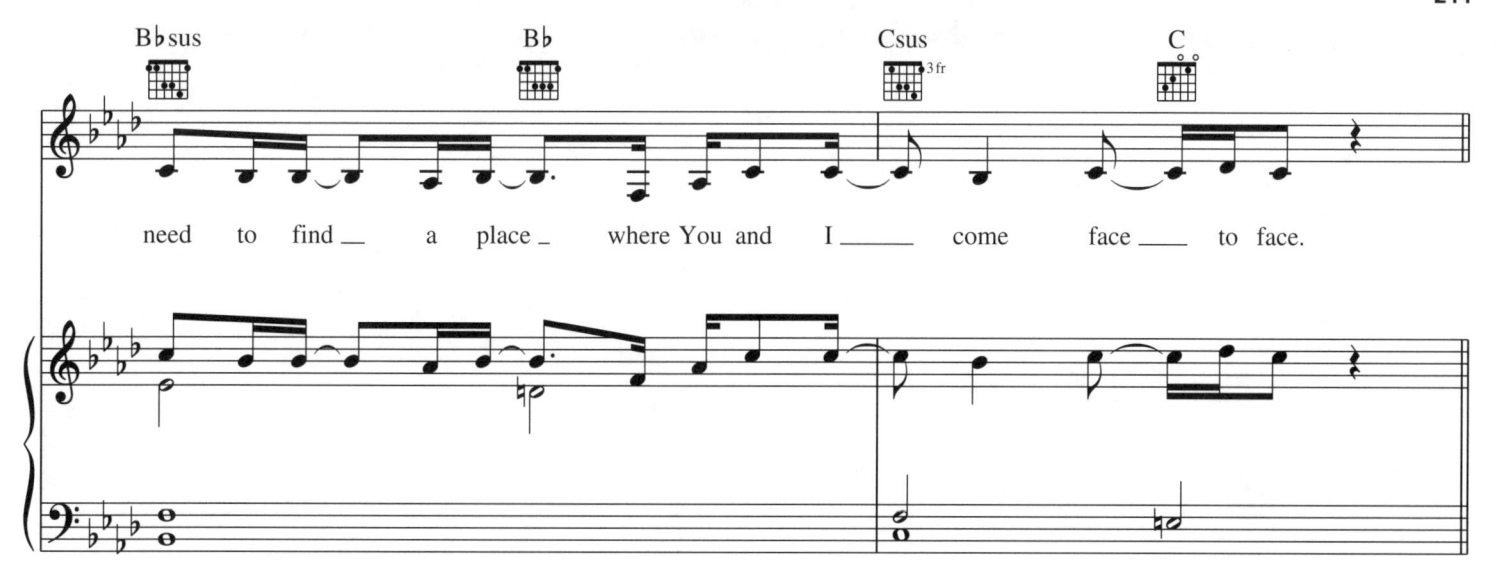

need to find a place where You and I come face to face.

Thomas needed proof that You had really risen
Nicodemus could not understand how You could

undefeated. When he placed his fingers where the
truly free us. He struggled with the image of a

nails once broke Your skin, did his faith fi-n'lly be-gin? I've
grown man born a-gain. We might have been good friends, cuz

lied if I've de-nied the com-mon ground I've shared with him. And I,
some-times I still ques-tion, too, how ea-si-ly we come to You. But I,

I real-ly want to know You. I

| Eb | Bbm | Ab/C |

want to make each day a dif-f'rent way that I can show You how

| Db | Ab |

(1.,2.) I real-ly want to love You.
(D.S.) I'm real-ly gon-na

Be

| Eb | Bbm | Ab/C |

pa-tient with my doubt; I'm just tryin' to fig-ure out Your

will, and I real-ly want to know You still.

1. still.

2. still. No more camp-in' on the porch of in-de-ci-sion, no more sleep-in' un-der stars of ap-a-thy.

D♭
A♭
4 fr
And it might _ be
B♭sus
B♭
C7sus
C7
ea - si - er ___ to dream, ___
but dream - in's not __ for me. ___ And I, __
D♭
D.S. al Coda
I real - ly want __ to know __
CODA
N.C.
real - ly want _ to know ___ You
D♭
A♭
4 fr
still. ___
I want to know ___ You, ___

real-ly want to know you.   Hey.

Hey.

I real-ly want to know You.   I real-ly want to know

217

WAIT FOR ME

Words and Music by
REBECCA ST. JAMES

Darling, did you know that I,___ I dream a-bout___ you? Wait-ing for the look in your

© 2000 UP IN THE MIX MUSIC and BIBBITSONG MUSIC (BMI)
UP IN THE MIX MUSIC Admin. by EMI CHRISTIAN MUSIC PUBLISHING
BIBBITSONG MUSIC Admin. by ICG
All Rights Reserved   Used by Permission

eyes when we meet for the first time.

Darling, did you know that I, I pray about you? Praying that you will hold on. Keep your loving eyes only for me. 'Cause I am waiting for, praying for you, darling. Wait for me, too. Wait for me as I wait for you. 'Cause I am

wait-ing for, pray-ing for you, dar-ling. Wait for me,

too. Wait for me as I wait for you. Dar-ling, wait.

Dar-ling, wait.

B♭7
E♭
Dar - ling, did you know I dream a - bout life to -
B♭(add4)/D
A♭(add2)
geth - er, know - ing it will be for - ev - er?
I'll be yours
B♭(add4)
E♭
and you'll be mine.
And dar - ling, when I say, "'Til death do us
B♭(add4)
Cm7
part," I'll mean it with all of my heart.
Now and al - ways

B♭sus
D.S. al Coda
faith - ful _ to you. 'Cause I am
CODA
A♭(add2)
4fr
B♭(add4)
3fr
_ I wait _ for you. Dar - ling, _ wait. _
D♭sus2
4fr
A♭(add2)/C
8fr
Bmaj7
Dar - ling, _ wait.
B♭(add4)
3fr
D♭sus2
4fr
Now, I know _ you may have made mis - takes, _
A♭(add2)/C
8fr
A♭(add2)
4fr
but there's for - give - ness _ and a sec - ond chance. _ So

B♭sus
A♭(add2)
4fr
B♭sus
wait for me, dar - ling, wait for me. Wait for me,
A♭(add2)
4fr
wait for me. 'Cause I am
F
C(add4)
wait - ing for, pray - ing for you, dar - ling. Wait for me,
Dm7
B♭(add2)
C7sus
too. Wait for me as I wait for you. 'Cause I am

F
C(add4)
wait-ing for, pray-ing for you, dar - ling.
Wait for me.
Dm7
too.
Wait for me as
1
B♭(add2)
Csus
3fr
I wait for you. 'Cause I am
2
B♭(add2)
Csus
Dm7
Csus
I wait for you. Dar - ling, wait.
Dar - ling, wait.
B♭(add2)
Csus
Dm7
Wait for me.

225

WISDOM

Words and Music by
TWILA PARIS

Moderately slow groove

I see a multitude of people,
There is a moment of de - ci - sion,

© 1999 ARIOSE MUSIC and MOUNTAIN SPRING MUSIC
Admin. by EMI CHRISTIAN MUSIC PUBLISHING
All Rights Reserved   Used by Permission

some far a-way _ and some _ close by.
but all the days _ go rush - ing by,

They weave to-geth - er new re - li - gion _____ from ti - ny rem-
an un - der-cur - rent of con - fu - sion _____ to threat - en all _

- nants they _ have found, _ a bit of truth, _ a great - er lie. _
_ that we _ be - lieve, _ with lit - tle time _ to won - der why. _

And all the proph - ets stand _ and sing _ a pleas - ant song, _
And all the proph - ets sing _ the same _ fa - mil - iar song; _

Fm7
Bb
Eb/G
3fr
a mil - lion cords _ that bind _ the spir - it grow - ing strong. _ My heart is
e - ven _ the cho - sen can _ be led ___ to sing _ a - long. _ These hearts are
Absus2
4fr
Eb/Bb
6fr
Bbsus
break - ing, I must re - mind them:
break - ing, will you re - mind us:
Eb
3fr
You are the on - ly way, _ You are the on - ly voice, _
Cm7
3fr
Ab
4fr
You are the on - ly hope, _ You are the on - ly choice. _

229

You choose the simple things to overcome the wise. Wisdom is granted in the name of Jesus Christ, in the name of Jesus Christ. You are the only way,

231

You are the only voice, You are the only hope,
You are the only choice. You are the one true God,
no matter what we say. You are the breath of life,
we need You here today. You are the only way.

You are the on - ly way. Give us wis - dom.

Give us wis - dom.

Optional Ending

Repeat and Fade